Football

A HISTORY OF THE PROFESSIONAL GAME

Football

A HISTORY OF THE PROFESSIONAL GAME

BY PETER KING

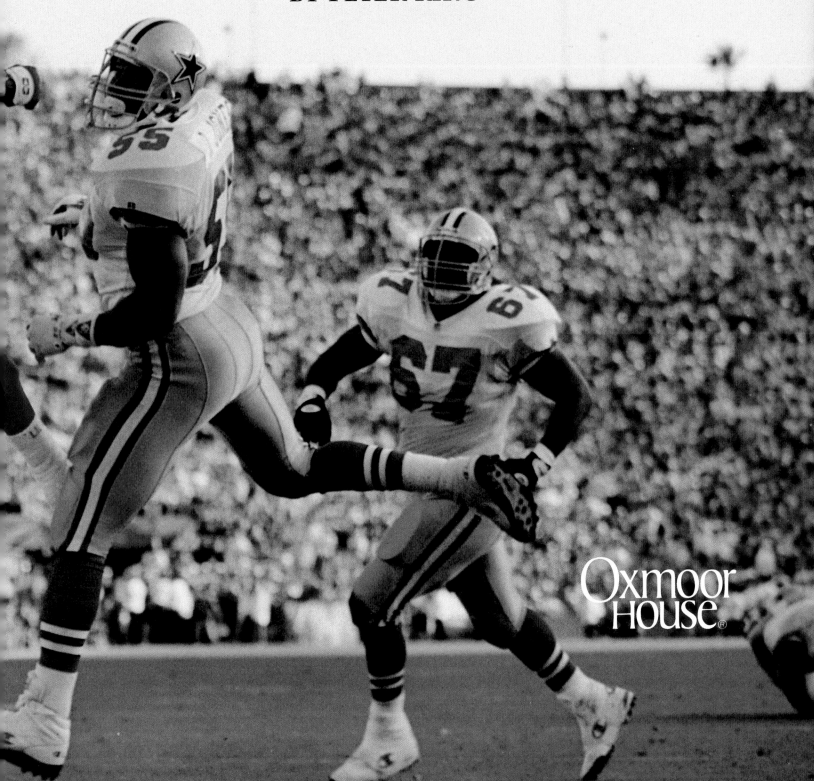

Oxmoor
House®

Copyright 1993
Time Inc.

SPORTS ILLUSTRATED is a
registered trademark of Time Inc.

ISBN: 0-8487-1168-8
Library of Congress Catalog Card Number:
93-085397

Manufactured in the United States of
America
First printing 1993

Published by arrangement with
Oxmoor House, Inc.
Book Division of
Southern Progress Corporation
PO Box 2463 Birmingham, AL 35201

Manager, Sports Illustrated Printed
Products: STANLEY WEIL

FOOTBALL: *A History
of the Professional Game*
Project Director: MORIN BISHOP
 Senior Editor: MERRELL NODEN
  Copyreader: LESLIE BORNSTEIN
  Reporter: JOHN BOLSTER
   Photography Editor: JOHN S. BLACKMAR
Production Manager: ANDREW HUGHES
Designers: STEVEN HOFFMAN
        BARBARA CHILENSKAS

FOOTBALL: *A History of the Professional Game*
was prepared by
Bishop Books, Inc.
611 Broadway
New York, New York 10012

Cover photograph (Larry Csonka):
Neil Leifer

To order SPORTS ILLUSTRATED
magazine, write to:
SPORTS ILLUSTRATED,
Subscription Service Department
P.O. Box 60001,
Tampa, Florida 33660–0001

CONTENTS

BEGINNINGS

I WAS LIKE YOU, OR MOST OF YOU, BEFORE I AGREED TO WRITE THIS
BOOK. I WAS DEFINITELY NOT A HISTORY GUY. I WILL CONFESS THAT
I KNEW SOME HISTORY. I SAW *JFK*. I KNEW HUGH BEAUMONT PLAYED
WARD CLEAVER. THE EXTENT OF MY FOOTBALL HISTORY KNOWLEDGE?

On my twelfth birthday, in 1969, I started to get *Sports Illustrated* at home in Connecticut, and the first issue was the one with Joe Namath on the cover, crying at having to choose between playing pro football and keeping his Bachelors III saloon in New York. NAMATH WEEPS, the cover hollered. That's where my knowledge of pro football history began.

That's why this book was a ball to write. I write weekly about pro football for *Sports Illustrated* now, but my root system stank. What did I really know about Red Grange? Who was Pudge Heffelfinger? And the Oorang Indians? Who won the Sneakers Game? Who knew?

It's amazing how little most of us know about the history of the most popular sport in America. And apparently, how few of us care. In my four years at the magazine I haven't received a single letter asking whether I really thought Jim Thorpe was over the hill when he became the Oorang Indians' player-coach. History bores people. I'm still not much of a history guy, but I am a pro football history guy. There are so many downright quirky things about the early days of pro football, like:

•The first pro game. No one is certain if the match between the Pittsburgh and Allegheny athletic clubs in 1892 was the first in which players got paid. But the game was a bitterly fought one, because the heads of both athletic clubs had competed fiercely to buy the services of the best player of the day, former Yale football standout Pudge Heffelfinger, a 6' 3", 200-pound mass of muscle. The Allegheny Athletic Club won Heffelfinger's services, for $500, and the investment paid off handsomely: In the 15th minute Heffelfinger recovered a fumble and ran 35 yards to score the game's only touchdown—and only points. The conversion kick failed. A touchdown in those days was worth four points, so AAC won 4–0. Literally, Heffelfinger was a hired gun, brought in for one game. A ringer.

•The Oorang Indians. In 1921 a dog-lover named Walter Lingo asked Jim Thorpe, then the president of the American Professional Football Association, to start a pro football team in the tiny western Ohio town of LaRue. Lingo would pay Thorpe $500 a week, but there were two catches. One: He wanted Thorpe to field an all-Indian team. Two: He wanted the all-Indian team to run his dog kennel and raise his favorite breed of dog, the

Heffelfinger, the former Yale standout, was a highly sought hired gun in professional football's first game in 1892.

Thorpe's duties with the Oorang team included the care of Airedales.

Airedale. Lingo thought Indians and animals shared a special, almost supernatural bond, and he thought he could sell his dogs for a higher price, as much as $500, if they were trained by real American Indians. In June 1922, at the same league meeting where the APFA was renamed the National Football League, Lingo paid $500 for an NFL franchise in LaRue, naming it the Oorang Indians because his favorite Airedale was named King Oorang. Recruiting on reservations in the Midwest, he came up with players named Lone Wolf, Eagle Feather, Running Deer, Red Fox, Bear Behind and Wood Chuck. And don't forget Long Time Sleep. He generated one of the earliest halftime shows ever by wrestling live bears. But the Indians won only three games in two years, and Lingo, beset by financial problems, had to dump the team and the players after a 1–10 start in 1923.

•The grueling itineraries of the pioneer pro teams. In 1930 the Green Bay Packers had a three-game, seven-day road trip to the East Coast. They took a train to New York and played the Giants on a Sunday, took another train to Philadelphia for a game with the suburban Frankford Yellow Jackets that Thursday (dressing in a nearby firehouse) and then rode the train back to New York. On Sunday, in full uniform, they took a bus from their hotel in Manhattan to the southern tip of the island. They took the ferry to Staten Island, got off the boat and walked a mile to the football field. They beat the Staten Island Stapletons 37–7 and then followed the same itinerary in reverse: walk, ferry, bus. The following day they took a train home to Green Bay.

•Red Grange's role in saving pro football. This is such a crazy, compelling story that I called a

Grange: The man who saved professional football?

writer friend of mine and a book agent friend and tried to pitch them a book on Red Grange, "The Man Who Saved Pro Football." Because he probably did. No money in it, the agent said. Understand that in 1925 Red Grange and Babe Ruth and Jack Dempsey were the biggest sporting names of the day; college football was the pinnacle of the sport, and the pro game was strictly bush league. In 1925, just days after being signed off the Illinois campus, Grange suited up for the Chicago Bears and began a 19-game, 66-day barnstorming tour of America, taking pro football to the big cities it hadn't touched yet and to cities where the game was struggling. In New York, in the Giants' first season, owner Tim Mara used to send his kids to school on Manhattan's Upper West Side with their pockets filled with tickets to give away, and very few of their classmates wanted

them. The Giants would have died without the Grange visit, Mara said later. Grange drew 73,000 to the Polo Grounds. Babe Ruth came to see him. President Calvin Coolidge beckoned him for a visit when the tour whistle-stopped in Washington, D.C. Grange drew 78,000 to the Los Angeles Coliseum. This was a big sport when Grange got through with it.

See what we have been missing? All this stuff is buried in the archives of the Pro Football Hall of Fame in Canton, Ohio. I've read Westbrook Pegler on Grange. I've held original letters from Pop Warner and Amos Alonzo Stagg. I've unearthed the incredible story of the Oorang Indians. I've read all the microfiche on Don Hutson, the greatest player in pro football history.

So get busy. Turn the pages. You've got a root system to develop.

ELEMENTS

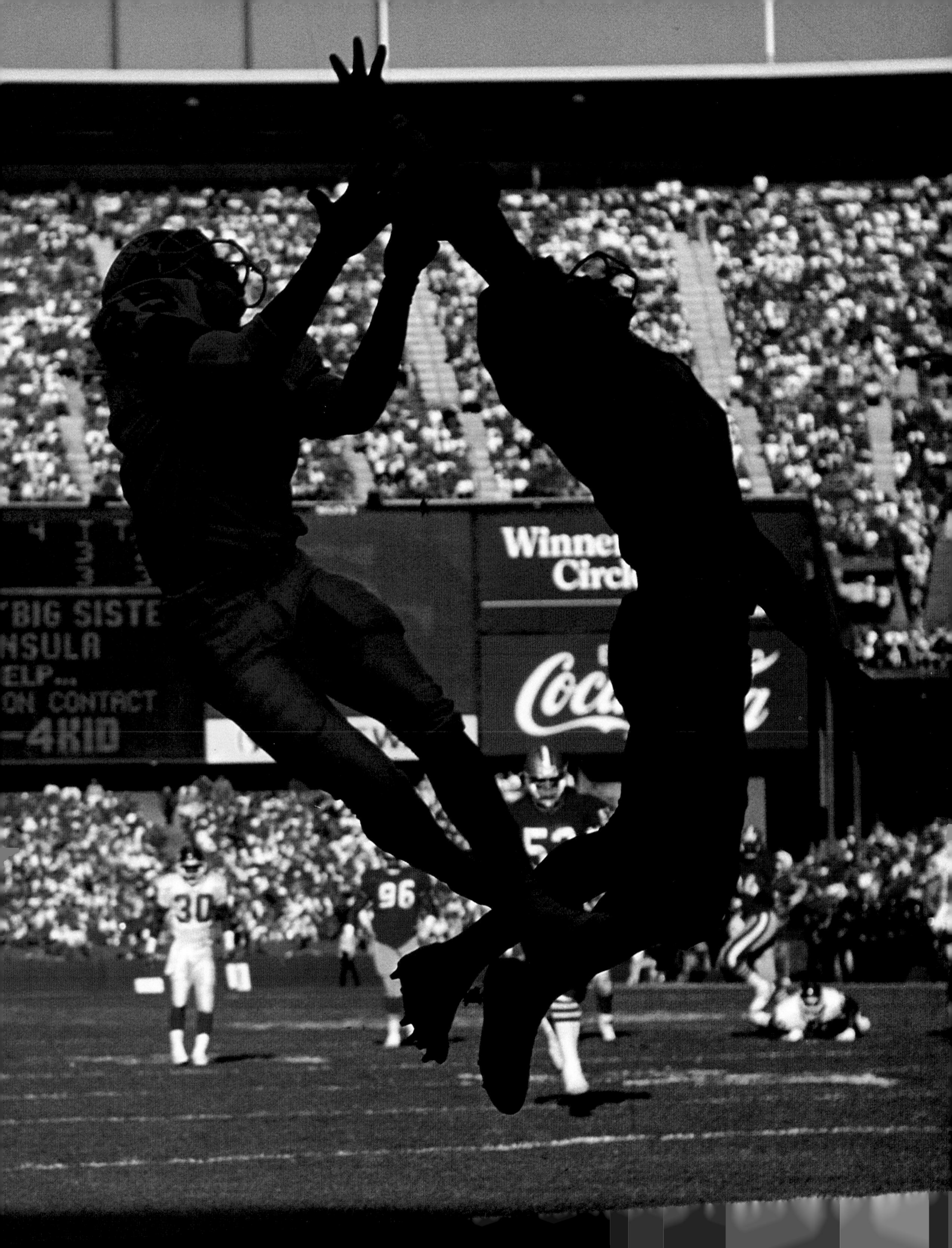
Winne
Circl
BIG SISTE
NSULA
ELP...
ON CONTACT
-4KID
Coca

The Run

Would you believe that the ground game in football is 170 years old?

That's right. There is a venerable school in England called the Rugby School, where for centuries lads have been hitting the books and the rugby fields with equal ardor. At the start of the 19th century the rules of rugby permitted players to throw or kick the ball to teammates, but it was heresy to run with it. In a match in 1823, Rugby student William Webb Ellis grabbed the ball and took off with it, neither kicking nor passing. Poor Ellis earned a severe upbraiding from school authorities because this clearly wasn't the proper way to play the game. Gradually, though, the rigid rules of rugby were relaxed to allow more of the students' athletic talents to show, and by 1846 it had become legal to run with the ball in a rugby match.

The British took the game to the Canadian maritime provinces, and it soon spread to New England colleges. Rules were improvised in those days; the game was different from one campus to the next. When two schools played, they had to agree on common rules. At Harvard a player could run with the ball if he were being chased, which was usually the case, and this custom spread. As a

Detroit's Barry Sanders: one of the most talented current practitioners of the art.

13

result running was a common feature of intercollegiate football in the 1870s. In 1874 Tufts, playing three half-hour periods with 15 men to a side, beat Harvard with a rushing touchdown. In 1876 Yale student Walter Camp, trying to run for a touchdown, lateraled the ball when tackled, and the new ballcarrier, Oliver Thompson, ran for the winning touchdown. Camp, of course, went on to become one of the chief architects of the college game.

Though the pass showed up every now and then as a blip on the football radar screen, running the ball quickly established itself as the way to survive and win in professional football. Paul Brown won very big on all three levels—high school, college, pro—with a dominant running game, and the offensive philosophies of coach after coach have favored the ground game. New York Giants coach Bill Parcells was echoing conventional wisdom when he said, in 1987, "Three things can happen when you throw the ball, and two of them are bad." At least Parcells had the good sense to build a passing offense that could win games when his running game failed, an occurrence other coaches of contending modern teams have failed to plan for. Jim Mora of the Saints and Marty Schottenheimer of the Chiefs have traditionally had strong defenses and good running games. But

when the run failed and they had to throw, the Saints and the Chiefs came up empty.

In recent years the trend has been toward versatile backs. Thurman Thomas of the Bills will make the Hall of Fame because he can catch as well as he can run. Ditto Roger Craig. "The game's changing," Craig said, "and now backs have to be versatile or they can't work in this league. When I came into the league a back could be one-dimensional and carry a team's load for years. But when I came in, I had to learn to catch, and my first few years in the league I was a fullback, blocking a lot. Then I moved to running back. I might not have been as talented as some backs, but because of all my experiences, I was versatile enough for the 49ers to use me where they wanted, when they wanted."

Indeed, the contemporary running game is as versatile as the men who execute it. The Giants won Super Bowls with four basic running plays; the 49ers had dozens. You can challenge teams who know just what you're going to do, or you can trick them with finesse blocking and unpredictable running. Bright as he may have been, William Webb Ellis can't possibly have imagined where his daring run would lead.

Jim Brown ran with an unstoppable combination of speed and power.

The Pass

Ah, Walter Camp, that old sage. In 1886 Camp, the former Yale player and future father of foot-ball, wrote a book called *Foot Ball: How to Coach a Team*. In it Camp observed that because everyone wanted to play running back, one of the keys to building a successful club was finding players who were willing to perform the unpleasant chores of blocking and passing.

"There are ten men eager to make a brilliant run to every one willing to pass the ball to another, better situated for carrying it ahead," Camp wrote. "Selfish men can be taught to play an unselfish game, but they are not reliable in a great match and before an enthusiastic crowd."

Probably it's asking a lot of the great inventor—which Camp most certainly was—to expect him to be prescient, too. How can he have known what was coming? Nowa-days, from the time a baby can say Joe Montana, his dream position in any pickup game or on any for-mal team is quarterback. Actually Camp's book has a terrific chapter on the responsibilites of the quar-terback. "If he executes his part of the play and the rest of it fails, he must receive the blame," Camp wrote. "It is only by this almost unfair treatment that he can be

The powerful arm of Denver's John Elway produced several miraculous comebacks.

17

taught to exercise the very best judgment on all occasions.... Place plenty of reliance upon him, but let him understand that this reliance necessitates his knowing everything that is transpiring as well as making some use of that knowledge."

Curly Lambeau must have met Walter Camp somewhere. Lambeau, the Green Bay Packers' founder and original coach, was the first football architect who believed that the quarterback was a team's most important player and that the forward pass was his most dangerous weapon. Lambeau himself quarterbacked the Pack in the early 1920s, completing 37 of 45 passes in one game. Later he took pedestrian players like quarterbacks Arnie Herber and Cecil Isbell and taught them to win with the pass. And he plucked Don Hutson off the Alabama campus in 1935 and made him the receiving cornerstone of the Green Bay offense. Hutson was the best player of all time—you can look it up, page 100!—and if you still don't believe it, you'll surely have to agree that Hutson was the outstanding player of his time, consistently making more catches for more yardage than any of his peers.

Lambeau viewed himself not only as a club executive and coach but as a salesman for the sport. He would tell the other men who ran football clubs in the 1920s and '30s: If we

don't make the game exciting, we'll all be out of jobs soon. Lambeau's Packers used this wide-open philosophy to win 212 games and lose 106 in his 29 coaching seasons.

Today the scientifically controlled passing game rules the day. The long throw is used not just as a weapon in itself but also as a means to soften up a defense and make it more vulnerable to the medium-range precision strikes. Bill Walsh brought this consistent, land-acquisition passing style to the NFL in 1979 with San Francisco, and the 49ers continue to use his coaching tapes to teach new players and coaches, even though Walsh hasn't coached the 49ers since 1988. Seven of Walsh's disciples—or disciples of disciples—entered 1993 at the controls of NFL offenses. Although the prevalent wisdom still says that a quarterback needs to have a powerful arm, the greatest quarterback of our time, Joe Montana, has a downright mediocre arm, and he became famous throwing 15-yard out patterns. Walsh sounds like a Camp guy when he says, "Give me a quarterback with physical tools, but also give me a quarterback who's very smart and who knows the best way to win games every Sunday. That's the quarterback I want."

The little-used Max McGee grabbed seven passes for Green Bay in Super Bowl I.

19

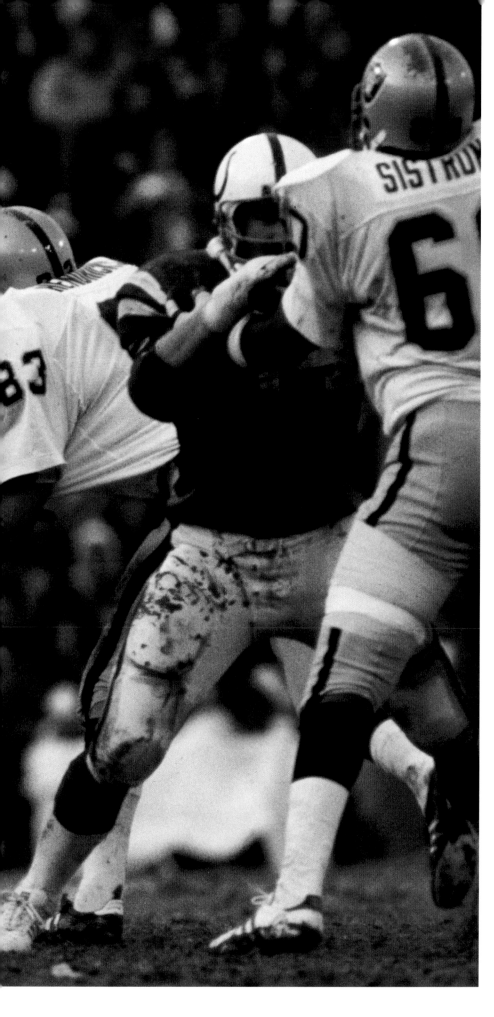

The Block

Back in 1879, when a football game was still very much like a rugby match, players at Princeton introduced a novel concept. Instead of attempting to advance the ball by clumping bodies together in a scrum and trying to overpower the other scrum, the Tigers tried to set the ballcarrier apart from the scrum. The ballcarrier, the Princeton brains thought, would be better able to make long gains by running free with two guardians on either side of him. One problem, fellas: What about the tacklers in front of the runner? The Tigers didn't take those guys into account, and thus very seldom were runners able to break for long gains. That's one good reason why Princeton struggled offensively that season and tied Yale 0–0 in the unofficial collegiate championship game.

Indeed, this game was so boring that it might have brought about the demise of rugby-type football. The way to show fan displeasure in those days was to hiss, and accounts of the game agree that there was a great deal of loud hissing that day. The 7,000 people who watched Princeton and Yale in Hoboken, N.J., that Thanksgiving Day saw very few runners break away from the pack. The scrums ruled the day.

Classic pass blocking gave Baltimore's Bert Jones a well-secured pocket on this play.

Eight players lined up in front of the ballcarrier in a 3-2-3 formation and tried to overpower the opposing scrum. The running backs, *The New York Times* observed in its account of the game, were often "nothing but interested onlookers."

The problem in those days was that football was a student game, run by students and coached by students and played by students; there was no father figure or respected architect of the game. Walter Camp, seeing how crowds and even players were turned off by these boring games, pushed through a new rule at a meeting of college football teams in 1879. The most important rule change in the history of the sport, it specified that the offensive team would line up across a scrimmage line from the defensive team and give the ball to a ballcarrier on every play. The ball was in play until the runner was tackled. No more 10-minute scrums. The ball would be hiked or kicked to the running back, and the defense would try to rush through the blockers to get to him. Blocking became less a leaning and pushing of a mass of bodies, and more of an individual, *mano a mano* contest.

Let's move ahead a change-filled 11 decades. Along the way offensive

Pulling guard John Niland (76) showed Dallas' Calvin Hill the way to daylight.

linemen have learned distinctly different techniques for pass and run blocking. They have also learned the fine art of "pulling," that is, leaving their position and leading a ballcarrier through a designated hole. But those changes were really only the beginning. If the blocking techniques of the 1880s were an abacus, those of the 1990s would be solar-powered calculators.

A couple of years ago I sat in on a Cincinnati Bengals' offensive line meeting and they might as well have been speaking Russian. They spoke of T bubbles and 19-calls, rake steps and Gilligans and line splits. And then there were hours of films. Hours. And then more hours.

"We're students almost as much as we are football players," Anthony Munoz, one of the greatest tackles ever, told me that day. "So much of blocking now is mental preparation, knowing what the guys across the line from you are going to do. And they're doing the same thing as we are right now, studying the same way. So it becomes a chess match as much as a physical power struggle, really."

The science of the game, to be sure, has changed. But one thing has remained the same: The biggest bodies on the line of scrimmage usually rule the day. Football is still a game of brute force, even with the pads and the helmets.

The Tackle

A century ago, in football's prehistoric days, the school fathers at Harvard were so alarmed by the game's full-speed, no-equipment tackling, by its brawling and cheap-shotting, that they did something that almost brought the game to a halt. They condemned it. They tried to have it banned from the Harvard campus, reasoning that Yale and Princeton and the other colleges that played the game would follow suit. The game, the Harvard professors wrote, "is brutal, demoralizing to teams and spectators, and extremely dangerous." It may have been. But the Harvard players were so anxious to play that they made a huge concession: They played all their games on the road that season.

No one could blame the intelligentsia, really. The rules at the time permitted pulling and punching and gouging and stopping the ballcarrier any way a player could think of, no matter how cruel or unusual. This wasn't exactly what the English had had in mind when they imported a rugby-type game to the Canadian maritime provinces decades earlier. They thought it was enough to stop the ballcarrier. Hard tackling was an American innovation, introduced into college football in the 1870s and '80s.

Punching may be illegal today, but being tackled can still be a brutal experience.

The real change in stopping ball-carriers—tackling—came about because of presidential intervention. In 1904, 19 players around the country died in football games. President Theodore Roosevelt decided enough was enough, and he summoned college football leaders to Washington, D.C., for a conference. Change the rules, he ordered them. Make the game less violent.

More penalties were added to the rule book. Officials were expected to be more vigilant about what happened after the tackle, on the bottom of pileups. Players began wearing more than padded leather hats and flimsy thigh pads to protect themselves against the rough tackling.

Why is it not surprising to learn that boys insisted on being boys and that the rules of the day were widely flouted? When George Halas signed Red Grange in 1925 and put him in a Bear uniform, Grange promptly learned how rough the pro game could be. In college the officials protected ballcarriers as best they could, calling penalties for slugging and throttling, so the players had a kind of guardian angel looking out for them. But not Grange. Writing in the *Chicago Tribune*, Westbrook Pegler gave this account of a game between the Bears and the Giants, held on December 6, 1925:

"Deep in the second quarter, as he knocked down a Giant pass, Red was slugged with a Firpoesque slam of the back of the headgear by Williams of the Giants, who had been sent out to receive the throw.... Williams, who learned his rough ways at Lafayette College, wound up like an old barroom fighter throwing the 10-pound cuspidor, and let Grange have it. Red stumbled unsteadily but did nothing about it, and neither did the officials, who were about as hostile to fist-fighting as Tex Rickard is, all afternoon. After he returned to the game in the fourth quarter, Tex was kicked on the forearm by Tomlin, and it wasn't long after that till Joe Alexander, the Giants' center, stopped him in a line play and squatted on the ground with Grange in his lap, trying to twist his head off to see what kind of sawdust he's stuffed with. The officials told Alexander he oughtn't to do that but didn't charge him anything for it."

The size and speed of the athletes today means tackles are harder to make and more crushing when made right. That is simple physics. "After a normal season," Giant quarterback Phil Simms said a few years ago, "I usually feel O.K. about April. Maybe May. That's how long it takes all the hits and the tackles from the previous season to go away."

Beware the blind side: a lesson Bart Starr is about to learn from Ordell Braase.

The Equipment

In the days before lights and stadiums and shoulder pads and helmets, there was one piece of equipment in a football game: the football.

It was a smooth, fat, oval thing, fatter than the streamlined, pebble-grained ball of today. And it often found itself in the middle of a pile of bodies with nothing but skin and clothing touching it. No shoulder pads, no high-tech helmets, no heavily insulated pants—such luxuries had no place in the early rugbylike form of American football.

Princeton's lone game of the 1873 season was at Yale—the Princeton kids made the trip by sailboat—and it was a terrific struggle. Early in the game, before either team had scored, a sound like a gunshot emanated from the field, and the players leaped back. Was someone shot? Who would shoot a firearm near a football field anyway?

The ball had burst.

A messenger was dispatched to a shop in New Haven to get another ball, and the game went on after a half-hour delay. Darkness ended the game prematurely, with Princeton declared a 3–0 winner, following one of the weirdest delays-of-game in football history.

The uniform and padding evolved

Could Red Grange (far right) and his mates imagine the changes to come?

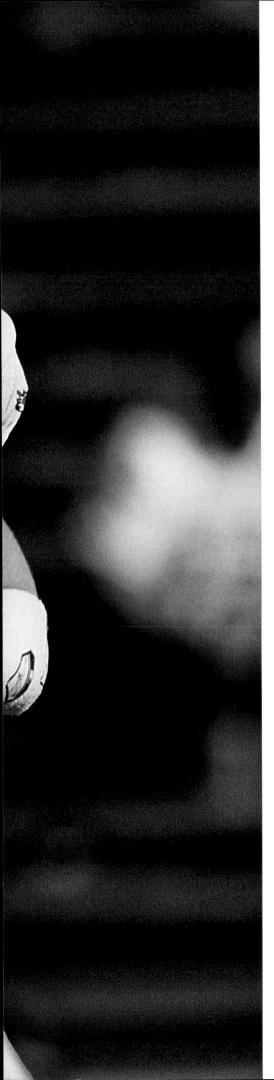

slowly. Like hockey goalies, football players weren't scared by the fatal facts of their lives, such as the 19 football players who died in 1904 alone. "Our suits were furnished by the players and were quite a collection of different styles," said Tuffy Conn, who played for the professional team in Massillon in 1917. Conn's "head guard," as he called it, was a leather hat with no padding. He bragged in his later years about getting tackled hard out of bounds by Jim Thorpe, smashing through a picket fence and careening into the grandstands. It was a macho thing. The padding wasn't necessary. They could take the hits. Even when Conn was in on a tackle that injured Thorpe's back, there was no call for more protection. There was only a call for visitors in the hospital. Thorpe told Conn he wanted to see him every day.

But by the 1930s thigh and shoulder pads were commonplace, worn by every NFL player. And the leather helmet started getting more padding. Every player wore a helmet by the end of the '30s, and most players wore spiked shoes designed specifically for football.

Since the 1930s the biggest changes have come in helmets and shoes. The evolution of the helmet

Face mask, tinted visor, thick pads: Jim McMahon epitomized the high-tech player.

has been incredible, from the hard plastic shell of 40 years ago to the spaceman's headgear today. Inside each helmet are inflatable pockets of impenetrable air-filled plastic. Each time a player puts on his helmet now, a trainer can insert a needle into the top and pump up the air pockets if the helmet is too loose. They're something like those shoes you personally pump up before you play basketball. The modern helmets, basically, are hard sneakers for the head. Of course, given the faster, stronger players of today, and the tendency to use the helmet as a weapon rather than as a piece of protective equipment, even more work is needed to guarantee protection from the terrifying sort of spinal injury suffered by the Jets' Dennis Byrd in 1992.

And the shoes. Some teams bring three or four different types of shoe per player to road games. The shoes have varying lengths of cleat—or no cleats at all, only treads. I once looked into Lawrence Taylor's locker at Giants Stadium and found an array of more than 30 pairs of shoes, with every conceivable variety of cleats and treads. Taylor took out the oldest-looking, most worn-out pair in the pile. He slipped them on almost like you would slip on loafers. What's the best equipment for a player today? The equipment that feels the best.

The Formation

In the beginning, there was a book, and the book was thorough. Written in 1893 by a group of authors that included Amos Alonzo Stagg, *Treatise on American Football* outlined 69 plays, many of them out of the classic T formation. The T positioned a player, known as the quarterback, behind the center, and on either side of the quarterback placed two backs, known as the running backs. Amazing how simple, and how familiar, things were a century ago.

Last spring Joe Horrigan, the historian and curator at the Pro Football Hall of Fame, was showing me some old letters from Amos Alonzo Stagg and Pop Warner, and he had a word of caution: "Remember," Horrigan said, "when all these letters appear in the '20s and '30s, and you have coaches claiming that they were the first to do something, they usually weren't. Most of the plays and formations are very old."

Most of the formations we see today, in fact, originated between 1890 and 1920. It's stunning to learn that the pro game had almost nothing to do with their development—though not quite so surprising when you consider that there was no pro football of note until the 1920s. In 1890 the coach at Yale, Walter Camp, began taking a guard

Lambeau used Hutson (with ball) to create a more wide-open passing game.

out of the T formation and sending him around end in front of the rusher, running interference for him. Thus was born the pulling guard. In 1900, at the Carlisle School in Pennsylvania, Pop Warner shifted his backs before the snap of the ball. Illinois coach Bob Zuppke ran the flea-flicker out of the T in 1906. Warner perfected the reverse in 1911.

The pros took these developments from the college game and improvised on them. In 1935 Green Bay coach Curly Lambeau spread the field with two wide receivers, including Don Hutson, and gave the passing game a bigger role. When the Bears were preparing for the NFL title game in 1940, coach George Halas invited Stanford coach Clark Shaughnessy to Chicago for a few days to work with his boys on perfecting the straight T. The result was a 73–0 win over the hapless Redskins.

But the game turned conservative for much of the next 20 years, and the next major offensive revolution occurred in the '60s, when Sid Gillman and Al Davis began to spread the field with a wild vertical passing game. In the 1980s coach Mouse Davis brought the run-and-shoot (one quarterback, one back, four receivers) into the United States

Richard Dent (95) and Gary Fencik (45): two of the hitters in the Bears' fierce 46.

Football League, and it had an aborted run that ended with the Lions in 1992. The Oilers are still successfully running a slightly more conservative version.

On defense, by contrast, there wasn't nearly as much innovation in the early days. The most intriguing developments have come recently, through the emphasis on rushing the passer. In 1984 Chicago defensive coordinator Buddy Ryan used his "46" defense to catapult the Bears to NFL prominence. In the 46, as many as eight defensive players crowded the line of scrimmage and tried to rush the quarterback chaotically. "All I want," Ryan would explain, "is somebody to go get the quarterback. I don't care who it is. But if the quarterback gets it in his mind that we're coming, and he's not going to have time to get the ball to one of his guys, then half our job is done. He's not thinking about playing the game. He's thinking about escaping from us. I like that."

With the Eagles' great defense dismantled for a variety of reasons, the best defense today is probably played by the Cowboys, who use 18 or 19 players interchangeably, hoping their 19th guy is fresher and better than the other team's 11th guy. But as football develops, it often seems that the best teams are the ones with the best benches... regardless of the formation.

The Kick

The act of kicking an oval ball for sport is at least 818 years old. We know this because some British scholar has unearthed a book called *History of London*, written by William Fitzstephen in 1175, in which Fitzstephen gives this memorable account of one popular recreation of the day:

After dinner, all the youth of the city go to the fields of the suburbs and address themselves to the game of football. The scholars of each particular school have their peculiar ball, and the particular trades have theirs. The elders of the cities, the fathers of parties, and the rich and wealthy come to the fields on horseback in order to behold the exercise of the youth....

And so it went for centuries, young people kicking and throwing oblong balls. The first placekick on record occurred in the 1882 Yale-Princeton game, propelled from the foot of a 158-pound Princeton guard named Jerry Haxall. Eyewitness accounts state that Haxall kicked a 65-yard "goal," which is hard to believe, since the NFL record for a field goal is 63 yards. But who knows? Modern isn't always best. Some of the greatest inventions appeared decades ago.

Roy Gerela (10) kicked a pair of field goals for the Steelers in Super Bowl X.

Still, for the most part, dropkicking ruled the day in early football; place-kicking was a novelty.

Soccer-style kickers began surfacing at U.S. colleges in the late 1950s and '60s. The Gogolak brothers—Pete with the Giants, Charlie with the Redskins—were the first proponents of kicking soccer-style. Just as the dropkickers switched to placekicking to gain accuracy, so did the straight-ahead kickers evolve into sidewinders. A soccer-style kick is, on the average, exceedingly more accurate than a straight-on one. Just look at the great kickers of the last 40 years, when the field goal has become a great weapon. Straight-ahead George Blanda has the second-most field goals ever; he hit 53% of them. Then came Jan Stenerud, who dominated the 1970s. Stenerud made 67% of his kicks. Now the alltime leader in field goal percentage (with a minimum of 200 field goals made) is Nick Lowery of the Chiefs. Lowery has been successful on 80% of his kicks. "Kicking," he says, "has become as much a science as any position."

But a discussion of the kicking game must include some words about the special teams. Los Angeles Ram coach George Allen lost a late-season game that cost his team a playoff spot in 1968 because the Rams had

Barefooter kickers like Denver's Rich Karlis have become commonplace.

a kick returned for a touchdown on them. So what did he do? He hired a young, energetic college assistant, Dick Vermeil, and made him the guru of his kicking teams.

That was the first step in the rapid modernization of the kicking game. Now they are called special teams, and most coaches think that special teams are as crucial to winning as offense and defense are.

"*More* important," says Buffalo coach Marv Levy. Levy coached the special teams under Allen, too. "When you realize how many plays a game are spent with kicking or punting teams on the field, and you realize how much yardage is exchanged because of the play of special teams, you sit back and realize just how crucial they are."

In 1991 the Giants beat Buffalo 20–19 in the Super Bowl. Giant coach Bill Parcells spent the last 20 minutes of his team's final practice simulating and then countering the way Buffalo special teams ace Steve Tasker chased down punts. In the game Buffalo's Scott Norwood missed a 47-yard field goal with eight seconds remaining, which would have won it. Looking back on the game, Parcells agreed that four of the five or six most valuable players on his Super Bowl–winning team were Matt Bahr, Sean Landeta, Reyna Thompson and Dave Meggett—all special teams guys.

The Culture

Pro football culture? I could bore you with stories about my childhood and the family trips to old Yankee Stadium, but I'd rather tell you about two recent "snapshots" of the game's culture. Both of them took place since I came to *Sports Illustrated* in 1989 and both of them happened outside of stadiums.

One occurred on a Sunday morning in 1990, as I drove behind the Chicago Bears' team buses on a four-lane state road from their hotel in Appleton, Wisconsin, to Lambeau Field in Green Bay, through rolling farmland. Up on the right, from about half a mile away, I could see a huge stuffed black bear, and as I got closer, it came into focus: It was maybe five-feet high, three-feet wide, with a face that looked very much like the logo of the Bears. It was hanging from a maple tree, with a rope tied around its neck, maybe 50 yards from the shoulder of the road. And just as the Bear buses sped by, two kids in the yard took to beating on the stuffed Bear. I mean, they were swinging at the poor thing like Cecil Fielder at a fat fastball, connecting with the guts and the head and the paws of the bear, and I thought, Boy, these people take this Bear-Packer rivalry seriously. I mentioned this scene to some tailgating Packer

Yankee Stadium, the author's source of memories, is a football mecca no more.

40

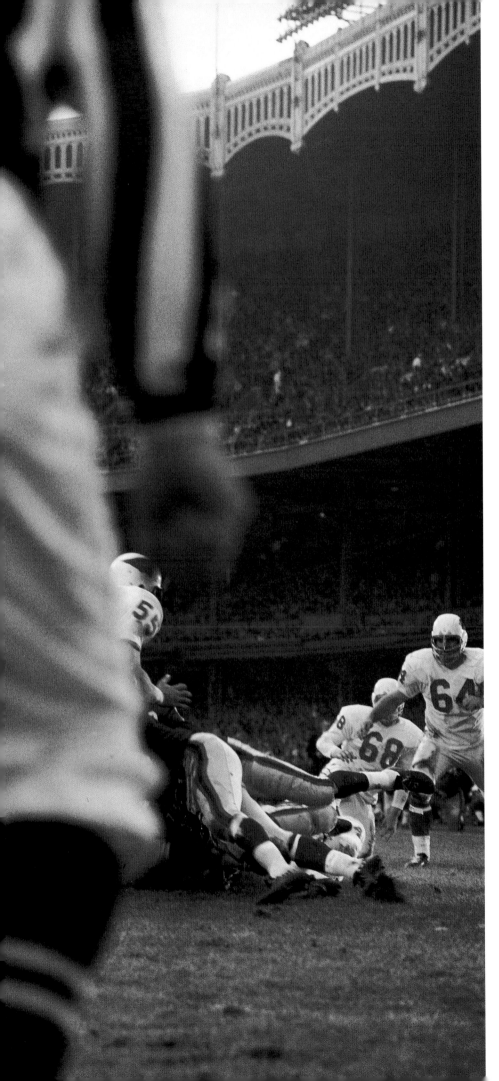

fans near Lambeau Field—you walk from your car through lots full of bratwurst-cooking tailgaters in Green Bay—and they smiled. "Two rules about being a Packer fan," one guy said. "You gotta love the Packers, and you gotta hate the Bears."

The other happened late one night in eastern Nebraska or western Iowa, I forget which. I was taking the Madden Cruiser across the country with the nation's most famous bus rider, John Madden, who, because of a fear of flying, takes a plush bus from one CBS-TV game to another each fall football week. It was one in the morning, and Madden was doing the usual—watching videotapes of one of the teams, Dallas, he would be seeing that week. "See," he said, alternately chewing on a cigar and taking long pulls of spring water from a 50-ounce bottle, "they can't ruin this game. No matter what they do to it, it's such a great game, with great games and great people in it, that no matter what anybody does, they can't ruin it." And he went on, waxing lyrical about the sport we flock to.

He's right, by any measure. Players can be paralyzed, and we watch. Steroids can pump up guys artificially, and we watch. Owners can line their pockets, and we watch. In the past five years the Harris polling group has surveyed Americans four times about their favorite sport, and four times pro football has won.

The NFL is corporateball. No question about it. The Super Bowl is ridiculously commercial, but the top 10–rated sports events on TV in U.S. history are Super Bowls. Eight of the top 10 shows ever are Super Bowls. Scar it, step on it, fight about it. No matter. People love it.

There's a load of dime-store-shrinks' theories as to why this is. We love the violence, as long as we're removed from it. We love to see people, legally, beat the tar out of each other. We like to like what other people like. Do I buy all this? I don't know. I think a lot of football's popularity has to do with the anticipation of the game, the buildup to a big game, the waiting. And the sociability of it. You can be an island and sit home and go nuts in front of your own TV, or you can go to a sports bar and flick your eyes from game to game on a Sunday. Or you can go to the stadium, if you're wealthy enough and fortunate enough. You walk through the parking lots at Lambeau Field in Green Bay—where tailgate heaven surely is, with what must be the greatest smell of all time, the bratwurst and the crisp fall air and the leather from the footballs whacking off the cars— and you think, Madden's right. No one can ruin this.

Television and professional football: a love affair that is likely to endure.

GAMES

Greates *I* Games

BALTIMORE 23
NEW YORK 17
(OVERTIME)

DECEMBER 28, 1958 The greatest game ever? It certainly didn't start like it.

One of the first nationally televised pro football games, in fact, looked a bit like a loser as it unfolded. The Colts lost their final two regular-season games on the coast to the Rams and the 49ers. The Giants beat the formidable Browns on successive Sundays prior to this game, once to tie for the Eastern Conference title and then to win it, but their mighty defense was battered heading into this world title game with the Colts. A gray, damp day and a New York newspaper strike held the crowd down, and, incredibly, there were 6,000 empty seats in Yankee Stadium, meaning that the game couldn't be televised in the New York area.

On the first series of the game, Baltimore quarterback John Unitas fumbled. On the second series, New York quarterback Don Heinrich was intercepted. On the third series, Unitas was intercepted. On the first scoring chance, Baltimore kicker Steve Myrha kicked a 24-yarder wide, but the Giants were offside. Then Myrha had his kick blocked by Sam Huff.

Game for the ages? Nah. More like a reservoir of punch lines for Jack Paar.

But remember one thing about that game and that day: There were 15 future Hall of Famers on the field. They had some classic football, lots of it, left in them.

Late in the third quarter, with Baltimore up 14–3, Colt coach Weeb Ewbank eschewed a chip-shot field goal from the New York four because of Myrha's troubles earlier, and running back Alan Ameche got dragged down on the Giant five. Back came the Giants, scoring on their next two possessions to take a 17–14 lead, which they held until late in the fourth quarter. They would have held it forever had not a freak play—keyed by a broken leg—brought the Colts back into it.

The Giants had the ball on their own 40, facing a third-and-four situation. There were three minutes left. Frank Gifford plunged into the line, apparently just shy of the 45, but surely enough for the first down. As he fell, so did Baltimore defensive end Big Daddy Lipscomb, right onto the leg of Colt Gino Marchetti. Marchetti's leg snapped. In the ensuing confusion, with a stretcher and medics running on and off the field, the ball was misspotted—or so the Giants claimed. And they were five inches short of a first down. "I know I made that first down," Gifford swore years later. But they had to punt, and

*Great blocking created a huge hole for
Ameche on the winning play.*

46

with 116 seconds left in regulation, the Colts took over at their 14, still trailing 17–14. America edged forward in its stuffed chair, waiting.

Unitas threw incomplete on first down. Unitas threw incomplete on second down.

On third down he found running back Lenny Moore for 11 yards, saving the drive. But the Colts were still 75 yards away. Unitas saw the Giants' coverage flooding the sidelines, so he decided to focus on the middle of the field. He hit Ray Berry for 25, and again for 15, and again, in the middle of two Giant defenders, for 22, to the Giants' 13. The clock ran. And Myrha, finally making a clutch kick, hit the tying field goal with seven seconds left.

In overtime, with a third-and-15 from the Colt 36, Unitas came up big again, throwing 21 yards to Berry, who caught an amazing 12 passes for 178 yards that day. Baltimore moved to the New York one, where Ameche smashed behind right tackle into the end zone.

Football is the megasport it is today because of games exactly like this one—one of the first seen coast-to-coast, exposing fans to the drama of football when it is played at its very best, with great players playing great football under great pressure.

"It's the greatest thing that ever happened," a breathless Berry said after the game. We're not arguing.

New York 16
Baltimore 7

JANUARY 12, 1969 If ever there was an allegorical game for a generation, this Super Bowl in Miami was it. Baltimore was the Nixon White House, the confident collection of pinstripe suits coming off a 13–1 regular season and a 34–0 whipping of Cleveland in the NFL Championship Game. Their quarterbacks, Earl Morrall and John Unitas, each had Haldemanian crewcuts. Their league, the National Football League, was so slick, so polished, so cocksure. And it had every right to be: NFL teams had beaten AFL teams by a combined 68–24 in the first two Super Bowls.

The New York Jets were Woodstock. Call them Country Joe (Namath) and the Fish. The Fu Manchued Namath, the true star of his sport, said what he wanted when he wanted, and he was the hero of the counterculture sporting scene. The Jets were good, with a fine powerback in Matt Snell and a productive wideout in Don Maynard, but they had struggled to a 27–23 win over Oakland in the AFL title game at home. The oddsmakers took one look at the game and said, Colts by 18.

Joe Namath took one look at the game and said, "We're going to win Sunday. I'll guarantee you."

Namath guaranteed victory, then went out and produced it for the Jets.

Truth be known, the NFL hated the AFL. The establishment hated pushy radicals like Al Davis and Joe Namath and even radical play-callers like Sid Gillman, the mad offensive scientist who would coach San Diego, Houston and the Rams. It just wasn't the NFL way to do what Namath did the Thursday before this game. At an AFL dinner where the drinks flowed freely, Namath was handed the league's Most Valuable Player trophy and asked to say something. Putting down his napkin-wrapped drinking glass, Namath gave one of the most discombobulated acceptance speeches ever. It went like this, in part:

"This isn't an award for me.... This should be a Most Valuable Player award for the entire team. You can be the greatest athlete in the world, but if you don't win those football games, it doesn't mean anything. And we're going to win Sunday. I'll guarantee you. When we won the AFL championship, a lot of people thanked the wives. I'd just like to thank all the single girls in New York. They deserve just as much credit. They're appreciated just as much." He took a sip of his drink. "You fellows out there under 21, this ginger ale is good stuff. But I'd like to clear something up right now. Some people seem to think that I drink J&B Scotch. That's not true; it's Johnny Walker Red ..." And so on.

Today every media opportunity at the Super Bowl is closely controlled. But then an oiled and swim-trunked Namath held daily briefings on a lounge chair wedged into the sand at the Galt Ocean Mile Hotel. "We're a better team than Baltimore," he said more than once. The NFL gritted its conformist teeth, but Namath proved he was right.

Snell rushed for 121 yards and would have won the MVP award were it not for Namath, who commandeered the Jets to a 16–0 lead before the Colts scored a meaningless fourth-quarter touchdown. Whenever the Colts blitzed, Namath had an answer; he completed 17 of 28 passes, for 206 yards and no touchdowns or interceptions. Who can forget the slump-shouldered Namath, a single digit puncturing the night sky, clumsily jogging off the field after the game? No words needed. The Jets were the best, and Namath had stunned the establishment into a grudging acceptance of the guys from the wrong side of the tracks.

Afterward veteran Jet safety Johnny Sample pulled a tattered newspaper clipping out of his wallet. It was a year old, he said. The headline read: LOMBARDI SAYS AFL INFERIOR.

"What's the headline tomorrow?" Sample crowed.

Namath's gesture as he trotted off the field said it all: The Jets were No. 1.

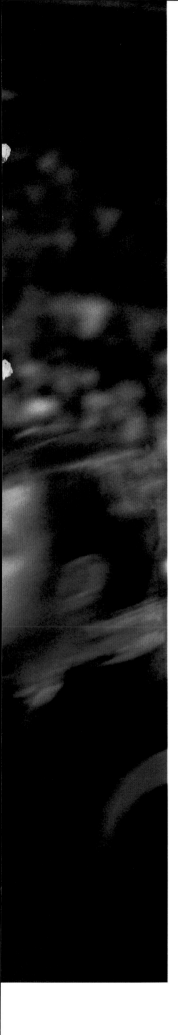

Greatest  Games

Chicago 9
Portsmouth 0

DECEMBER 18, 1932 In 1932 there was no official NFL Championship Game, there were no hash marks on the pro football field, and passes had to be thrown from at least five yards behind the line of scrimmage. Players often got IOUs instead of paychecks, it being the Depression, and hard times had shrunk the league from 18 teams in 1922 to eight a decade later.

This was a game in trouble.

A snowstorm and a circus helped save it.

Every game has its magic early moments, times that helped make the game what it is today. This was football's. Pro football's, especially. The pro game hadn't even taken a backseat to the college version yet; the professional players were still stuck way back in the trunk. George Halas, the Bears' coach and owner, seven years earlier had helped boost the pro game's credibility when he enlisted Red Grange to tour with his team, but his acquisition hadn't quite cemented the new league's reputation. Now, late in the 1932 season, with Chicago and Portsmouth (Ohio) heading for a tie atop the NFL standings, the league's power brokers saw another opportunity to promote the sport: Why not arrange a championship game if the two teams finished the season with identical records?

Halas, league president Joe Carr and Portsmouth owner Harry Snyder all agreed, so the match was set for December 18 at Wrigley Field—if the two clubs indeed tied. And tie they did, at 6–1; the Bears had six ties and the Spartans had four, but the league called it a draw anyway. As the 18th approached, a snowstorm hit Chicago. By the time the Spartans got to a bitterly cold Chicago three days before the game, 18 inches of snow covered Wrigley Field. They would have to play indoors, Halas knew, or call off the game. Here's where the circus came in handy. It had just left Chicago Stadium, and six inches of dirt lay on the indoor floor. Halas threw some trucked-in sod on top of it, and presto! Instant field. It was only 80 yards long, though, and 15 yards narrower than the normal field, so the two teams agreed that any time the ball was spotted near the sideboards, it would be moved in 10 yards. That's how hash marks were born.

Chicago and Portsmouth had tied twice (7–7 and 13–13) during the regular season, and this game was deadlocked at 0–0 entering the fourth quarter. The Bears ran an interception back to the Portsmouth 13 with 11 minutes left. Everyone in the place knew the Bears would let ace back Bronko Nagurski try to stuff it in from there, and try he did. But his four carries went for six, five and then twice for zero yards. Third-and-goal from the two, and who took the handoff? Nagurski, of course. He rushed toward the line, suddenly stopped in his tracks, backpedaled and leaped into the air. This was no run! This was a jump pass, to Red Grange, standing alone in the end zone. No ref in his right mind could take this touchdown away—Nagurski to Grange, Legend to Legend, for the championship— even though the Spartans howled that Nagurski was closer to the line than five yards when he threw the pass. Chicago added a safety, and the 9–0 victory was history. Soon afterward the Bears were christened the Monsters of the Midway.

More than the nickname, though, the excitement of this game spawned the separation of the league into divisions; the Eastern and Western winners would henceforth meet annually in a league championship game. Passing rules were modernized, abandoning the arbitrary five-yard zone so that passers could throw from anywhere behind the line of scrimmage. And the league adopted hash marks, opening up the game offensively. Some very big things came from playing on that very small field.

A venue better suited to the circus became the site an historic football game.

Greatest 4 Games

BUFFALO 41
HOUSTON 38
(OVERTIME)

JANUARY 3, 1993 It was halftime of Buffalo's AFC playoff game with Houston, and Bill coach Marv Levy was angry. "Whatever happens, you guys have to live with yourselves after today," Levy spat out at his sullen team. Levy's Bills had just followed a 27–3 regular-season-finale loss at Houston with a horrible first half in front of the home folks in round one of the playoffs. Imagine Levy's anger when, at the start of the second half of the game, he looked out and saw Oiler safety Bubba McDowell returning an interception 58 yards for a touchdown. Houston now led 35–3, with 28 minutes to go. And Buffalo was without three of its cornerstone players: quarterback Jim Kelly (knee sprain), running back Thurman Thomas (hip pointer) and linebacker Cornelius Bennett (pulled hamstring).

Thirty-two minutes played, 32 points behind.

"We had a chance," Levy said, "about the same chance a guy has of winning the New York Lottery."

In the press box two Houston TV guys made nonrefundable airplane reservations for a trip the next week to Pittsburgh, site of the next round's game. A league official told Buffalo p.r. director Scott Berchtold sympathetically, "Well, you guys had a good run." In the stadium about

54

10,000 people walked out, cursing their Bills, many of them eschewing their postgame tailgate parties to start the long drive home. Who felt like a party after watching this shlock?

What followed was something like points raining from the sky, like something no one in the stadium—or no one in America, for that matter, watching their TVs in stunned disbelief—had ever witnessed before. No NFL team had ever come back from a thirtysomething-point deficit, and certainly not in a playoff game. "It was like time was standing still," said wide receiver Ernest Givins of the Oilers, "like they were scoring every 15, 20 seconds."

Maybe it was fortuitous that the Bills were forced to use backup quarterback Frank Reich. Before the game, eerily, Reich buddy Boomer Esiason, on the NBC pregame show, had warned the audience at home about what a great comeback quarterback Reich was, about how he had led the University of Maryland back from a 31–0 deficit to beat Miami in 1984. Back the Bills came behind Reich. While Houston's offense kept going three downs-and-out, Houston's defense and special teams went into deep-nap mode. Buffalo got 28 points in 11 min-

Kicker and quarterback—Christie and Reich—celebrate the incredible comeback.

utes—Kenneth Davis diving across from the one followed by three Reich touchdown passes. Houston entered the fourth quarter hanging on 35–31.

Fate entered the lineup then. With seven minutes left the Oilers lined up for a 31-yard field goal attempt with the wind at their backs. "Exactly then," Oiler holder Greg Montgomery said, "it started raining. The ref doesn't wipe off the ball—that's pretty standard procedure—and I yell to the ref, 'Hey, wipe it, ref!' And he says, 'Play ball!' Then, the snap's coming back to me, a little high, and a gust of wind blows it out of my hands."

Go figure. And while you're at it, figure out why Andre Reed of the Bills caught as many touchdown passes in the second half, three, as he had caught all season. The third put Buffalo up 38–35 with 3:08 left, and though Houston managed to send it to overtime, this one was over. Warren Moon threw an interception on the first series of overtime, and Steve Christie ended it with a 32–yard field goal.

"We choked as a team, choked as players, choked as management," Houston cornerback Cris Dishman, near tears, said after the game.

"We fight," said Buffalo linebacker Darryl Talley, "until they kick the last breath out of us."

These emotions happen in the greatest comeback in sports history.

Greatest 5 Games

GREEN BAY 21
DALLAS 17

DECEMBER 31, 1967 They played this football game without whistles. You know the little brown wooden balls inside some whistles? Well, these little brown balls, unable to stay loose with the temperature at −13° at Lambeau Field in Green Bay that Sunday, froze inside the officials' whistles. Of course, everything was freezing that day. Bob Lilly, the great Dallas defensive tackle, took a cup of water inside his hotel room that morning and threw it against the window. The water stuck there, frozen. And the 750,000-volt heating-coil system under Lambeau Field, to keep the field unfrozen, went out. Kaput. Stone-cold dead.

If the '60s Green Bay Packers are one of the greatest teams of all time— and they certainly are—then this was their signature game, on their home tundra. The talent-laden Cowboys were on Green Bay's tail through the mid-'60s, trying to overtake the Pack for NFL superiority. The Packers had won titles in both 1965 and '66, repelling the young Cowboys 34–27 in a thriller in '66. Now, in 1967, Dallas was trying to break through again, and their chances to do so seemed good. Early in the fourth quarter Dan Reeves threw a

Starr (15) burrowed through a tiny hole for the game-winning touchdown.

stunning 50-yard halfback option pass to Lance Rentzel, and the Cowboys led 17–14. "Oh my Lord, what have I done?" said Green Bay cornerback Bob Jeter, who blew coverage on the play.

Well Bob, there had to be a stage here and great drama, and we needed someone to set it up. You did.

And here came the Packers, from their own 31, with 4:50 to play. Quarterback Bart Starr kept hitting his backs, Donnie Anderson and Chuck Mercein (acquired on waivers from the Giants for $100 earlier in the season), with passes or hand-offs, and the Packers got to the Dallas 30 at the two-minute warning.

What a role the cast off Mercein played on this day. Green Bay was 30 yards away against a terrific defense, and Starr wanted to go to Boyd Dowler or Carroll Dale, his two wideouts, on first down. "But if the linebacker doesn't pick up Chuck coming out of the backfield," Starr said, "I hit him immediately. I saw the linebacker freeze, so I hit Chuck quick." For 19 yards, out of bounds at the Dallas 11.

Then, on first down, Starr called the perfect play. Lilly, the future Hall of Famer on the Dallas front four, had been giving young Packer guard Gale Gillingham all he could handle all day, so Starr called for Gillingham to pull as if the play were a sweep. Gillingham pulled, Lilly followed,

and Mercein shot through the gap for eight yards, to the three.

Three runs got the ball to the two-foot line. There were 16 seconds left. The Packers called their last timeout. It was third down. Coach Vince Lombardi could choose a safe pass in the end zone; if it failed, he could kick the chip-shot 18-yard field goal. If he chose to run, the Pack could be assured of getting only one play off. Surely Lombardi would leave himself the option of the kick, wouldn't he?

"I was thinking of the fans," he said later. "I couldn't stand to think of them sitting in those cold stands for an overtime period."

On the sidelines Starr told Lombardi, "I can sneak the ball in." Stunningly, Lombardi let him. "Wedge 30," Starr called in the huddle, which meant a handoff to Mercein, who would try to burrow in over right guard Jerry Kramer. Only Lombardi and Starr knew the quarterback would keep it. Kramer dug his right foot into an unusually soft piece of turf, and Starr lumbered in the little hole opened by Kramer. Starr was right. He could sneak it in, and he did.

"This game," weary Packer tackle Bob Skoronski said later, "was our mark of distinction." Years later, his words couldn't be truer.

According to Lombardi, his sympathy for the frozen fans made him gamble.

59

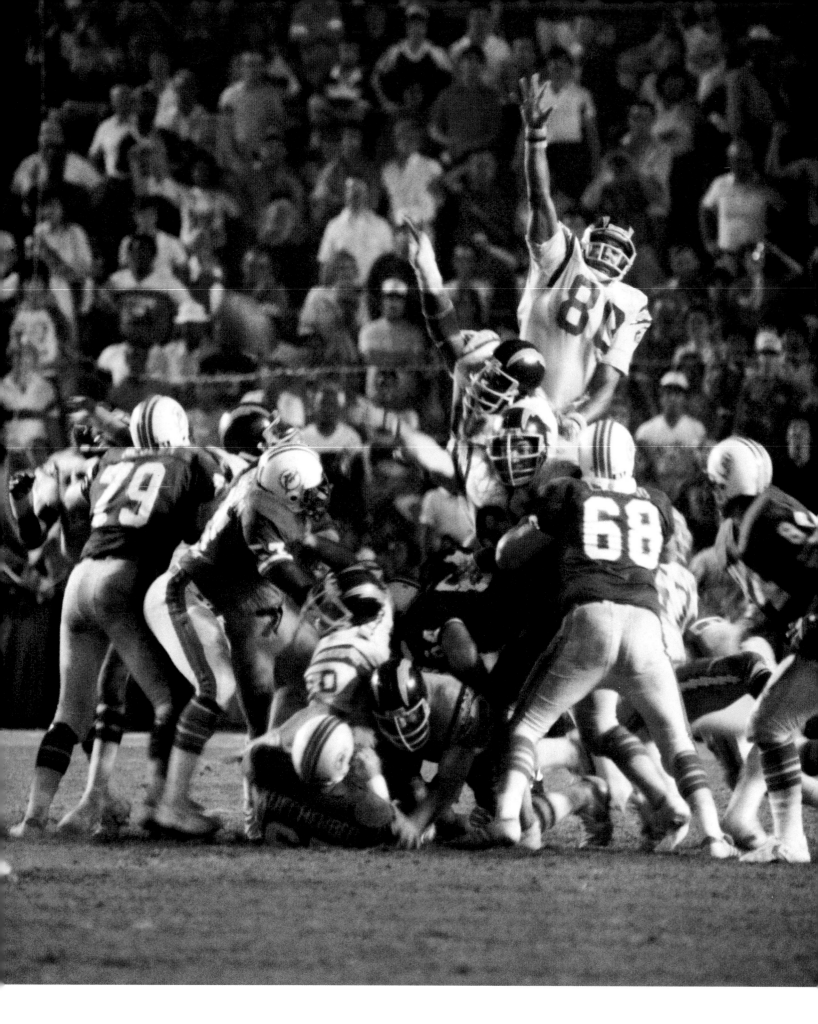

Greatest Games

SAN DIEGO 41
MIAMI 38
(OVERTIME)

JANUARY 2, 1982 For sheer back-and-forth drama, this might have been the most exciting pro football game ever played.

The Chargers scored 24. Then the Dolphins scored 24. San Diego got a touchdown, then Miami got a touchdown. Miami got a touchdown, and San Diego got a touchdown. At 38–38, Miami had a field goal attempt blocked, and San Diego missed a field goal; then Miami had another field goal attempt blocked, and San Diego, almost 14 minutes into overtime, finally made a field goal. "A Game No One Should Have Lost," was *Sports Illustrated*'s headline the next week.

San Diego's Dan Fouts threw for 433 yards. Miami's Don Strock threw for 403. It was the first time two quarterbacks had each thrown for over 400 yards in the same game.

Amazingly, though, with all the odd circumstances of this game—including oppressive heat (87°) and humidity—the most memorable thing was a tight end. San Diego's Kellen Winslow caught 13 drive-controlling passes for 166 yards. And he jumped three feet into the air to get his right hand on the potential game-winning

Winslow (89) rose above the crowd to block Miami's late field goal attempt.

field goal with four seconds left in regulation, swatting the ball away and sending the game into overtime. As he struggled off the field after the game, wobbly and spent, he yelled, "I feel like I've been to the mountaintop!"

To talk of just a few of the plays in this game is to do a disservice to the terrific ones we don't mention, but let us start with the last play of the first half. Miami ball at the San Diego 40, seconds left, Strock back to pass. He threw to wide receiver Duriel Harris on a 15-yard buttonhook, and as four Charger defenders converged on Harris, he did just what he was supposed to do on 87 Circle Curl Lateral: He lateraled to running back Tony Nathan at the 25, and Nathan pranced home. It was a game again, at 24–17. The Dolphins went 74 yards for the tying points on the first drive of the second half, and Fouts found Winslow alone in the end zone for a 25-yard score to make it 31–24. Strock hit no-name tight end Bruce Hardy for a 50-yard touchdown to tie it again. Fouts was intercepted by safety Lyle Blackwood, starting the Dolphins on the drive that would make it 38–31, Miami. Through it all Winslow kept leaving the game and coming back, because of a bruised shoulder and cramps.

Miami should have won it right here, because the Dolphins stopped San Diego again and started a grinding drive. But Charger linebacker Linden King stripped rookie running back Andra Franklin of the ball with three minutes left at the Charger 18. Fouts sprinted the Chargers downfield. At the Miami nine with 58 seconds left, Fouts looked for Winslow but overthrew him ... right into the hands of rookie running back James Brooks. Touchdown. 38–38.

Then came Winslow's block, and it was on to overtime. Fouts took the Chargers 79 yards with the opening kick, but Rolf Benirschke missed a 27-yard chippie. Strock took the Dolphins to the San Diego 17, where Uwe von Schamann scuffed the dirt on his approach and missed an easy 34-yarder. Mercifully, Benirschke hit the winner, from 29 yards, with 68 seconds left in the first sudden-death period.

Winslow, the conquering hero, had to be half carried off the field by two teammates.

"It's the closest to death I've ever been," Winslow said, gasping for breath after the game. And the closest to immortality.

Fouts threw for 433 yards, 166 of them on 13 passes to the ubiquitous Winslow.

Greatest  Games

DECEMBER 23, 1972 "Did you know," Terry Bradshaw said 20 years later, "that Art Rooney was in the elevator during the Immaculate Reception? Unbelievable. The owner of the team never saw it."

Well, Art Rooney wasn't alone, rest his soul. No one else saw it either. Bradshaw, the Steeler quarterback, didn't see the weirdest play in NFL history. The NBC crew doing the game didn't see it. NFL Films caught only glimpses of it. Some Raiders said they saw it, but the officials didn't believe their version. It's so steeped in mystery that, to this day, probably the only player who really knows the truth about the end of this game won't tell what he knows. Just what the game needs: an enduring mystery, with some of the biggest names in NFL history involved.

A quick briefing on the strangest end to a pro football game ever:

The first great Pittsburgh team of all time led most of the game, thanks to two Roy Gerela field goals. The Raiders finally took the lead, 7–6, with 73 seconds left, on a 30-yard touchdown scramble by quarterback Kenny Stabler, and that's how it stood, with 22 seconds left.

On fourth down. From the Pittsburgh 40. With the Steelers gasping their last breath.

Right about this time, with the Steelers in the huddle, Rooney, their cigar-chomping owner, boarded the elevator for a silent ride to the locker room. He wanted to get there when the players got in, to thank them for a great season and wish them a happy off-season. On the field Bradshaw got flushed from the pocket. He saw sub back Frenchy Fuqua wide open 20 yards downfield, and he fired, the hopes of a team and a city spiraling through the air. Just then he got leveled, and he never saw a thing.

At the same time the Raiders' brutal safety, Jack Tatum, sprinted toward Fuqua. Fuqua could hear the steps. He knew they belonged to Tatum. In a millisecond he could hear Tatum breathing. He knew his head was about to be knocked off.

The ball and Tatum arrived at Fuqua simultaneously, then the ball caromed crazily 15 yards away, and Franco Harris plucked it off the Three Rivers Stadium tartan turf and sprinted past the stunned Raiders, running 60 yards for the winning touchdown. Even before Rooney's elevator hit the ground, the crowd told him something incredible was happening.

It was, but only if the play was ruled legal. In 1972 a pass caroming off a player to a teammate was incomplete. "Tell them you touched it! Tell them you touched it!" Tatum yelled to Fuqua. Tatum claimed the ball never touched him. But Fuqua wouldn't say a thing. Hasn't to this day, in fact. Even when his old buddy Bradshaw asked him for the truth for the CBS *NFL Today* show in 1992, Fuqua played it coy and wouldn't say.

The officials wouldn't signal a touchdown. They wouldn't signal anything. Crew chief Fred Swearingen called upstairs to the league supervisor of officials, Art McNally, who confirmed what his crew was telling him: They all thought both Fuqua and Tatum had touched the ball. Swearingen hung up the phone, ran to the field and signaled touchdown. "This will hurt for a long, long time," Oakland coach John Madden said.

Thank goodness for Fuqua's love of controversy. Did Babe Ruth really call the World Series homer in Chicago? Did Frenchy Fuqua alone touch the ball? Hopefully, we'll never know. Mystery is good.

When Harris sprinted to victory, he set off an enduring controversy.

Greatest Games

Green Bay 35
Kansas City 10

JANUARY 15, 1967 A few days before the Packers, of the 48-year-old National Football League, took on the Chiefs, of the seven-year-old American Football League, Green Bay coach Vince Lombardi was feeling the heat. He couldn't lose. He just couldn't lose, not to these ... these ... upstarts. When Lombardi got to his hotel room one day after practice in California, there was a telegram waiting for him from league patriarchs George Halas and Wellington Mara. "We are proud you and the Packers are representing us, the NFL, in this first game," the telegram said, in part. Lombardi shuddered over the great expectations. A friend who was with Lombardi that week said 25 years after the game, "Vince couldn't sleep that week. He felt like the weight of the league was on his shoulders, like if he didn't win by four touchdowns, it wouldn't be good enough."

Green Bay safety Tom Brown knew. "We've just beaten Dallas for our second straight NFL championship," he said in the days before the game. "But you know something? If we lose this game, the season won't mean anything. If we lose, people will remember us as the NFL team that lost to Kansas City in the first game played between the leagues."

So the players felt the pressure too. Lombardi refused to train in Los Angeles for the game. The distractions would be too great, he figured. So they practiced 90 miles to the north, in Santa Barbara—until commissioner Pete Rozelle ordered the Packers to Los Angeles three days before the game. Seems the national press was hungry for tidbits in L.A., and the writers couldn't interview the Packers if they were 90 miles apart. Another oddity about this first game played with a Roman numeral following it: Both NBC and CBS telecast it. They were both willing to pay million-dollar rights fees for it, so the leagues figured, why not?

They paid all that money, and what they got for it was pretty good TV. Kansas City hung tough, holding Green Bay to a 14–10 lead at halftime. And when Kansas City quarterback Len Dawson got the Chiefs to midfield early in the third quarter, the crowd was warming up to the game. But then Green Bay safety Willie Wood intercepted a wobbly Dawson throw, running it back to the Chief five. Soon it was 21–10. Two drives later Bart Starr found hung-over wide receiver Max McGee for the

clinching touchdown. Green Bay, 28–10. In all, it was quite a day for McGee, who had enjoyed a long Saturday night out because he didn't think he would play much; he did, because of an injury to Boyd Dowler early in the game. McGee had caught four passes all season; against Kansas City's weak cornerbacks he caught seven passes for 138 yards and two touchdowns, his biggest game in years. "Green Bay picks out a weak spot and sticks with it better than anyone I've ever seen," said Chief running back Mike Garrett.

Taking advantage of a plethora of those weak spots, Green Bay coasted through the second half to win, and afterward Lombardi walked into the locker room clutching the game ball his players had given him. He had survived the challenge. He had won big, as he should have, and as everyone in the NFL prayed he would. In three years, the leagues would merge, and so the enmity of one league versus another would soon die. In three years Vince Lombardi himself would be dying of cancer. The game, and this spectacle, would get bigger, but it never would be quite the same without him.

Starr was his usual efficient self, completing 16 of 23 passes for 250 yards.

N e w   Y o r k   2 0
B u f f a l o   1 9

The Norwood miss produced a title for the Giants, dejection for the Bills.

JANUARY 27, 1991 In airports people pass through metal detectors before boarding planes. At some presidential speeches, SWAT-team snipers squat atop roofs, on the lookout for suspicious types. In cargo hangers dogs sniff out contraband or bombs. At political rallies waves of little American flags shake collectively in the crowd.

Metal detectors, sniffing dogs, crouching snipers, waving flags: These are things we have grown accustomed to in certain circumstances—but certainly not at an American professional sporting event. Not at least until they all came into play at this very strange, very patriotic, very exhilarating, very good Super Bowl for the ages in Tampa.

The NFL pulled out all the security stops for this one because of the threat of terrorism. We were in the middle of the gulf war then, and Saddam Hussein was a more feared player in this game than Thurman Thomas. "I thought terrorism was a real threat," Giant president Wellington Mara said later. It took 90 minutes to enter Tampa Stadium because of the long security lines, but 90 minutes can buy a lot of peace of mind. The stadium seemed safe, secure.

It was. Nothing but terrific football took place on this winter Sunday evening. In fact, the Giants were lucky to be there, having barely squeaked by the 49ers 15–13 in the NFC title game. Leaving Candlestick Park, coach Bill Parcells turned to offensive coordinator Ron Erhardt and gave him his marching orders for the Super Bowl: "Shorten the game." In other words, hang onto the ball as long as you can. Parcells had seen the first half of the AFC title game that day. Buffalo led the Raiders 41–3 at halftime on their way to a 51–3 final score. The Bills and their new no-huddle offense had scored 85 points in their first six playoff quarters. No wonder Parcells wanted to shorten the game.

Erhardt shortened it, all right. The Giants had the ball for 40½ minutes, long enough to build a 20–19 lead with 2:16 to go. Then the Bills took over at their 10, 90 yards from their first Super Bowl win in their first Super Bowl try. Buffalo quarterback Jim Kelly piloted the Bills to the Giants' 30, where, with eight seconds left and the clock stopped, Scott Norwood trotted onto the field to try the biggest field goal of his life. Of anyone's life, for that matter.

69

There hadn't been such a big kick—win if you hit it, lose if you miss—in any Super Bowl, ever.

You couldn't like Norwood's odds. His longtime regular holder, John Kidd, departed as a free agent for San Diego before the season, and he had had trouble acclimating himself to new holder Frank Reich; his longest field goal of the year was 48 yards; his field-goal percentage of .690 was the lowest in the AFC. As he lined up for the kick, the din in Tampa Stadium was absolutely oppressive.

Reich put the ball down. Norwood ran at the ball a bit too aggressively, and his plant foot, his left, went about five inches farther ahead than Norwood would have liked. The kick was long enough, but it was headed straight for the right upright.

And it tailed to the right by 24 inches.

On the Buffalo sideline grown men cried. As the Giants burst into their dressing room, the emotion rushed forth in torrents. Bill Parcells kissed Lawrence Taylor. He hugged sometimes-nemesis George Young, the club's general manager. The Giants were big kids, living big dreams.

But Scott Norwood was living a very big nightmare. He probably still is today.

Greatest Games

10

CHICAGO 19
NEW YORK 7

DECEMBER 6, 1925 For the entire autumn young Wellington Mara would go to his elementary school on the Upper West Side of Manhattan, pockets bulging with tickets. Even when Tim Mara's kid would give out handfuls of tickets to the newest game in town, Sunday would come and there would be a meager crowd at the Polo Grounds again. The New York Giants, the city's new professional football team, went 8–4 in its first year, 1925, but the fans stayed home in droves.

"The team was a financial disaster," Wellington Mara says now.

Indeed, the NFL fretted about the franchise, because an East Coast toehold was crucial if the league, then in its sixth year and still a largely midwestern phenomenon, was going to grow. But, truth be told, Tim Mara, who had bought the Giant franchise for $500 prior to the 1925 season, was thinking seriously of folding it after one season because the attendance and the attention were so spotty.

Grange (with ball) revived the flagging hopes of a fledgling league.

The pro game was struggling everywhere, in fact. Games weren't broadcast on the radio, and newspaper coverage was minimal. "Newspapers would throw our stories in the wastebasket when we'd send them over game information," Chicago boss George Halas said. "The college game was what everyone cared about." And the college game had one dominant force: Illinois

halfback Red Grange. In 1925 sports headlines around the country screamed about Babe Ruth, Jack Dempsey and Red Grange, and not necessarily in that order.

The week before Grange's 1925 college season ended, a promoter named C.C. (Cash and Carry) Pyle approached him and told him he could make a fortune by finishing the season with the Chicago Bears, then going on a barnstorming tour nationally. The only perk football had provided Grange up to that point—aside from his single room at the Zeta Psi frat house on the Illinois campus—was a free pass to the local movie house. So Grange played with the Illini at Columbus the following Saturday, November 21 (rushing for 192 yards, throwing a touchdown pass and intercepting another) and—voila!—there he was, five days later, on Thanksgiving Day, suiting up for the Bears against their city rivals, the Chicago Cardinals. The papers were flooded with Grange stories, and more people, 36,000, came to the game than had ever seen a pro game before.

Then came the Grange tour, which was a cross between a circus, professional wrestling and pro football. At one point Pyle scheduled eight games in eight

cities in 12 days. The tour went by train from the Midwest (the traveling Bears played a team of morticians in St. Louis) to the East to the South to the West Coast. The Bears played in a downpour in Philadelphia on Saturday, December 5, then washed their uniforms and took a train late that night for a game the next afternoon at the Polo Grounds.

What happened there was beyond Tim Mara's wildest dreams. "There is no doubt [Grange] saved the Giants," Mara said years later. The largest crowd ever to watch pro football, about 73,000, crammed into the Polo Grounds and on the bluff overlooking the stadium. The throng of common folk and celebrities—Babe Ruth stopped by the Bears' hotel to meet Grange, but no one's quite sure if the Babe made the game—wasn't disappointed. Grange, playing both ways as always, scored on a 35-yard interception for the final points in the Bears' 19–7 victory.

"Surely football would have caught on," Wellington Mara, the president of his dad's old team, says now. "But I don't know when, and I don't know how. This surely accelerated how quickly pro football became a national sport and a popular sport."

Greatest Games

DALLAS 17
MINNESOTA 14

DECEMBER 28, 1975 Your dynasty is aging in too many spots and fuzzy-cheeked in too many others. Bob Lilly and Walt Garrison have just retired. You have 12 rookies on the roster. The mix just doesn't seem right. You didn't make the playoffs in 1974, and you lost to Green Bay (4–10) and Kansas City (5–9), both at home, this year in the regular season, and you're starting to think: It's over. We won a Super Bowl, and we had fun, but it's over now.

You had to sneak into the playoffs as a wild card in a very weak NFC season, and now you go north to Minneapolis, into the tundra, against the best team the conference has to offer, with your graying quarterback unable to throw deep well because of badly bruised ribs, and everyone is saying this is finally the Vikings' year. And it should be, because their accursed quarterback, Fran Tarkenton, finally has a swell supporting cast.

And the game unfolds, and your guys keep it closer than you have a right to expect, but you watch as the Vikings, behind Tarkenton's scrambling and darting and mixing in a short pass here and

In spite of bruised ribs, Staubach completed 17 of 29 passes for 246 yards.

73

there, travel 70 yards early in the fourth quarter to take a 14–10 lead. (You hear later that Tarkenton's father, the Reverend Dallas Tarkenton, died about this time, of a heart attack as he watched the game at home on TV in Georgia.) And then it becomes a defensive game, until it's your ball, fourth-and-16 from the Dallas 25, with 44 seconds left.

You don't like your chances.

But your quarterback, the Navy hero, Roger Staubach, floats a pass to the right sideline for Drew Pearson. The ball hangs up a little too long, but Pearson catches it, flying through the air, and he's pushed out of bounds by cornerback Nate Wright at midfield. The refs give it to you, though the crowd is screaming because Pearson did come down out of bounds. First down, 32 seconds to go. Pearson asks for a rest, so Staubach goes elsewhere, while Pearson's chest heaves. Incomplete. "I can beat Wright deep," Pearson tells your quarterback, who breathes deep and grits his teeth because of the pain in the ribs. "Streak route," your quarterback tells Pearson.

Pearson sprints straight down the right sideline, and Staubach winds up and throws it as far as he can, a rainbow of a pass going deep and long toward the end zone. Wright stays with Pearson step for step until looking back for the ball at around the 10. You see the ball is going to be short, and both men slow up, and somehow, either by a push or by a slip—we'll never know for sure because everybody involved tells a different story—you see Wright fall to the mostly frozen earth. And at the five-yard line the ball hits Pearson near the crotch, and you see him gather it into his hands, and he lumbers the last couple of steps into the end zone, and you exult, because this was one you probably never should have won. Even your coach, Tom Landry, admits later, "Before that play, I was just standing on the sideline feeling very disappointed that we had played so well and were going to lose."

And you're proud of your team, because your long run should be over this year, but the team changes on the fly, and you watch as it makes the playoffs eight straight years after this one, and you wonder: Are we a charmed team? Are we blessed? Does somebody up there really like us? And did this game maybe mean a little bit more than just an impossible playoff win in the tundra?

And you think, yes, this is all true, and you're very happy to be a Dallas Cowboy fan.

Greatest 12 Games

Oakland 43
New York 32

NOVEMBER 17, 1968 Somewhere in an accounting of the most meaningful games ever, there has to be a game in which television was a factor, given the importance of that medium to the growth of pro football. We hereby nominate one of the great games of the '60s, the climax of which America didn't get to see because NBC, in the middle of a furious fourth-quarter rally, switched to the sight and sound of a young girl yodeling at a herd of European goats.

Ladies and gentlemen, meet the Heidi Game.

This game was a classic even without the yodeling. At a time when the American Football League was still striving to keep pace with the NFL, the two top attractions in the younger league were Oakland and New York. Indeed, this game would be a preview of the AFL Championship Game just six weeks away— and remember, the winner of that one would set the football world on its ear. Jets 16, Colts 7. On this day, for one rare time slot, the AFL game was killing the NFL game in the ratings. The AFL, indeed, had arrived.

The two most charismatic figures in the AFL were involved in this game. Joe Namath, leading the Jets to an 11–3 record, would be a run-

Much of America missed the game-winning dash by Oakland's Smith.

away AFL most valuable player. And Raider owner Al Davis, the architect of this team and its brazen image, was on the verge of winning Oakland's second straight AFL West title at 12–2, using every motivational trick he could dream up. The week before this game, in fact, someone in the Raider organization—wonder who?—posted a huge photo of Oakland defensive end Ben Davidson delivering a seismic blow to the side of Namath's face.

The game was everything they said it would be. The Jets, on two Jim Turner field goals, went up 6–0; the Raiders, on two Daryle Lamonica touchdown strikes, went up 14–6; the Jets, on two Namath scoring drives, went up 19–14; Oakland, on a Charlie Smith touchdown scamper and a two-point conversion, went up 22–19; the Jets, on 10 quick fourth-quarter points, went up 29–22; the Raiders, on another Lamonica touchdown bomb, tied it at 29; and the Jets, on Turner's fourth field goal of the game, went up 32–29 with 65 seconds left.

Whew.

NBC sighed then, at about four minutes to seven on the East Coast, because it needed to break for its Sunday night movie at seven. The Raiders couldn't move the length of the field and score, could they? America never saw. Oakland, driving after the commercial break, was at the Jets' 43-yard line with 50 seconds to play. And the next thing in living rooms up and down the East Coast was not Lamonica and Fred Biletnikoff and Davidson. It was Heidi and the goats and the Swiss Alps.

In New York the shouts went up

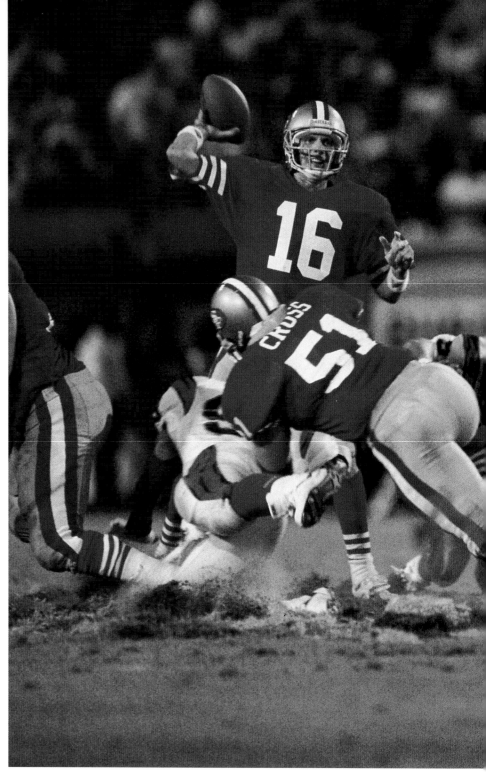

immediately. What is this little girl in pigtails doing on my TV screen! NBC phone lines were flooded.

On the next play Lamonica threw a short pass to Smith, who ran 43 yards for a touchdown.

On the next play the Jets fumbled the kickoff, and some Raider named Preston Ridlehuber recovered it and ran in for a touchdown.

Nine seconds. Fourteen points.

Raiders win 43–32. And no one in the five boroughs saw it. They were too busy throwing shoes at TVs.

The immediate moral, for network types, was: Never leave an exciting game for regular programming. The long-term message for the game was this: Football on TV had become so influential and such a sales tool, that football fathers would have to respect TV more than any other medium.

Montana worked his comeback magic
on a football field in shambles.

Greatest Games

SAN FRANCISCO 20
CINCINNATI 16

13

JANUARY 22, 1989 Strange week. Strange game. The Bengals were warned not to walk the streets around their hotel at night because of violence stemming from the anti-police bitterness in the black community. When John Madden's bus took a wrong turn in downtown Miami one night, it got stoned by angry youths, breaking windows on the Madden

Cruiser. The night before the game, Cincinnati's troubled starting fullback, Stanley Wilson, was found fried on cocaine in his hotel room. The league suspended him immediately.

But that same night something else quite significant happened. It had rained in Miami the day before the game, and the turf at Joe Robbie Stadium was too wet to leave overnight. So the NFL's grounds-keeper extraordinaire, George Toma, turned on the suction beneath the turf to suck the water down into the drainage system. He left instructions with the regular stadium turf managers to flip off the suction before leaving that night.

Uh-oh.

When Toma arrived on Super Bowl Sunday morning, he found the suction still on. They had forgotten to turn the thing off Saturday night. His heart sank. He stepped on the field. The grass was brittle, dying; the sod felt sandy to the touch. This field was so dry, Toma knew, that it wouldn't hold, that it was likely to come up in big chunks and strips. And it did. In fact, the poor footing led to a lousy three quarters of football during which Cincinnati built a slim 13–6 lead. The Bengals still led, 16–13 with 3:20 to go, when Montana took over on the crumbly field at his own eight. Jeez, this was almost too much time for classic Montana—if he could be classic Montana today. He hadn't been so far. He had completed 15 of his 27 passes. Nice, but hardly a dominant showing.

"We felt they had to go to the outside of the field," Cincinnati cornerback Lewis Billups said. "They didn't have time to use the middle of the field."

Yes, they did. At least Montana thought so. So did coach Bill Walsh. They used the middle of the field to chip, chip, chip away: eight yards to Roger Craig (clock moving), seven to John Frank (clock moving), seven

to Jerry Rice (clock moving), 17 to Rice, who stepped out of bounds (clock stopped), 13 to Craig. On second-and-20 from the Cincinnati 45, after a penalty, Montana took a huge risk. With Billups on one side of Rice and free safety Ray Horton on the other side and menacing strong safety David Fulcher prowling behind them, Montana called a 15-yard square-in to Rice. "It had to be a perfect throw and catch," Billups said, "because he had all kinds of hands flashing in his face." Boom. Perfect, for 27 yards. From the 18 Montana hit Craig right in the hands for eight more on a crossing route.

In the huddle before the next play, during a timeout, Montana took a minute to scan the crowd. "Hey

look," he said to center Randy Cross and a few others, "there's John Candy. Over there." Pretty cool fellow, this Montana. Now, with primary receiver Craig covered, he shot the ball inside Horton to an in-stride John Taylor. Touchdown. No sweat. Eight completions in nine attempts. Ninety-two yards in 2:46. Nothing to it.

"We had them on their eight with three minutes to go," Bengal receiver Cris Collinsworth said. "Somebody came up to me and said, 'We got them now.' I said, 'Have you taken a look at who's quarterbacking the San Francisco 49ers?' That's what it came down to. Joe Montana is not human. I don't want to call him a god, but he's definitely somewhere in between."

Craig was a key contributor to the game-winning drive, grabbing three passes for 29 yards.

Greatest 14 Games

MIAMI 27
KANSAS CITY 24
(DOUBLE OVERTIME)

DECEMBER 25, 1971 Years later Don Shula still couldn't believe what he saw that day. A nice NFL back—O.K., better than average—named Ed Podolak ran all over his Dolphins for 350 all-purpose yards. There were 85 yards rushing, 110 yards receiving and 155 yards returning, with two touchdowns. "Still haven't stopped Ed Podolak," Shula said years after Podolak's career ended.

Years later much of the NFL couldn't believe this game either. And it wasn't just because of the length of it. The Dolphins had never beaten Kansas City before this Christmas Day game. In six games the aggregate score was Kansas City 183, Miami 47; in four of those games the Chiefs had shut out the Dolphins. And this game would be at Kansas City, with the same basic cast for the Chiefs that whipped Minnesota in 1970 in Super Bowl IV.

The valiant Dolphins, with a miracle worker of a coach in Shula, had turned from a 3-10-1 team in 1969 to 10–4 in 1970 and 10-3-1 this season. Shula preferred a grind-it-out offensive style, using the powerful legs of Jim Kiick and Larry Csonka, to an air-it-out aerial style. But the secret of Miami's sudden offensive success was that Shula now had a passing game too as Bob

Griese and Paul Warfield became one of the league's most feared combinations. They were in perfect synchronicity on this very long day. Csonka and Kiick rushed for a combined 142 yards. Warfield had 140 receiving yards by himself. Griese threw for 263.

Yet the most important Dolphin of the day was a balding 5'7" chap from the island of Cyprus with the size-seven feet whose off-field business was painting neckties. I'll give you a clue: When the Dolphins flew back to Miami that night, he kept telling his adoring fans not to step on his feet.

"I knew we would win this game," Garo Yepremian, the kicker, said after the game.

Why?

"Because last night I was very good at cards. I say, 'When I win at cards, we win.'"

Oh.

Actually these teams were incredibly evenly matched. Both went 10-3-1 in the regular year and both had nearly the same number of first downs (Kansas City 23, Miami 22). Kansas City's apparent edge that unseasonably warm day was Podolak, who had run through the Dolphins all day and was threatening to keep going for the winning points on a kickoff return with about a minute to play in regulation and the score tied at 24. Podolak

burst through a hole in the Miami defense and ran until he had only Yepremian to beat. Yepremian, at about the Miami 40, made Podolak veer off-course so he lost his momentum briefly. And then Dolphin Curtis Johnson caught up to him and shoved him down near the Miami 22. Yepremian, Chief coach Hank Stram said later, saved a touchdown. But who was worrying? The AFC's Pro Bowl kicker, Jan Stenerud, who would finish his career in second place on the NFL's alltime scoring list, came aboard three plays later for a 31-yard chip shot. And the ball went a foot wide to the right.

New life. In the first overtime Stenerud had another chance, this time from 42 yards. And Nick Buoniconti blocked it.

"This is the worst day of my life," Stenerud said.

Yepremian soon had a shot from 52 yards out, but he pushed it wide to the left. He said later the miss gave him confidence, because he knew he had the distance to make a long one. Finally, 7:40 into the second overtime, almost 83 minutes into the longest game of our lives, Yepremian hit a perfect 37-yarder.

"I feel good for me," Yepremian said. Heroes usually do.

Csonka's second quarter plunge into the end zone brought Miami within 10–7.

Greatest Games

C L E V E L A N D 3 5
P H I L A D E L P H I A 1 0

SEPTEMBER 16, 1950 For four years the Cleveland Browns of the All-America Football Conference won every title their little league had to offer. But there was this one problem: The bigger NFL thought the AAFC was a bush league. "For four years," Brown lineman Lin Houston said, "we had to put up with being called a high school team with a high school coach. We were tired of that."

The Browns did have one of the most storied high school coaches ever. But Paul Brown, 81-7-2 in nine Ohio high school seasons, went on to coach a national championship team at Ohio State, and he had competed against and beaten the NFL in the race for several big-time players with his new postwar Browns in Cleveland. Finally, with the AAFC-NFL bidding war getting too rich for the blood of the NFL owners, the established league offered to take in Cleveland, San Francisco and Baltimore. Brown and his AAFC fellows agreed.

The NFL is famous today for choreographing a great matchup in 1970 to kick off the *Monday Night Football* season on ABC. In 1950 the NFL commissioner was Bert Bell, the former coach and owner of the Eagles and a native Philadelphian, so guess what he did? He matched his former team, the

defending NFL champion Eagles, with the defending champs from the other league, Cleveland, and put the game in cavernous Municipal Stadium the night before every other team in the NFL was due to open the season. Good planning. A huge crowd of 71,237 showed up for the clash of champions.

The Eagles were missing ace running back Steve Van Buren. Van Buren's backfield mate Bosh Pritchard was also injured. But fans in Philly still thought they would blow the rinky-dink Browns back to Ohio. In fact, no one was giving the Browns much of a chance, much like no one gave the AFL clubs much of a chance in the early Super Bowls. "I never said we could beat the best of the NFL," said Paul Brown at the time. "I never even said we could beat the worst. All I wanted was a chance, and now we have it."

The best quarterback of the day, Otto Graham, proved his worth this night. He shredded an Eagle defense that allowed a league-low 11.2 points per game in the championship season of 1949, throwing touchdown passes in the first, second and third quarters and running for a fourth score early in the fourth quarter. Cleveland's talented receivers, Dub Jones and the aptly named Mac Speedie, had their way with the Eagles' beleaguered secondary,

catching a combined 12 passes for 207 yards. At the end of three quarters the rout was just about complete: Cleveland led the Eagles 21–3.

And what a bunch of whiners the Eagles turned out to be. Coach Greasy Neale always complained that the Browns won so decisively because the Eagles were so beat-up that day. Nice logic, Greasy. You're playing at home, before more than 71,000 fans, and you lose by 25, and you're whining? Come on. You got whipped, and the Browns proved they belonged. One more petty thing: The Eagles allowed 346 passing yards by the great Graham, and they wondered if the Cleveland ground game was good enough to beat them. Well, when the two teams met 11 weeks later in Cleveland, Brown ordered Graham not to throw. The Browns ground out a 13–7 win.

In the locker room afterward a magnanimous Bell left no doubt he wasn't your average homer. "Cleveland is the best football team I have ever seen," Bell said. Quite right. The Browns were in the NFL Championship Game their first six years in the NFL. They won three. Their record says they must be one of the best teams ever to wear helmets. Ten seasons, 10 title games, seven titles.

Speedie was a marvel, grabbing seven passes for 109 yards and a touchdown.

16

Greatest Games

CHICAGO 73
WASHINGTON 0

DECEMBER 8, 1940 You don't have to be 70 years old to think this must be the strangest game in NFL history. You didn't have to be in Griffith Stadium three weeks before this game and watch the Redskins beat the Bears to know what a bizarre turn of events this was. You just have to be a thinking human being and consider a couple of facts. The Redskins went 9–2 to win the NFL Eastern Division in 1940. The Bears went 8–3 to win the Western Division. And here were the results in their head-to-head confrontations that season:

November 17, at Griffith Stadium—Redskins 7, Bears 3.

December 8, at Griffith Stadium—Bears 73, Redskins 0.

What is most remarkable is that the Bears, that day and years later, didn't seem to think a rout was ridiculous.

Eating breakfast with a local reporter at Washington's Willard Hotel that morning (my, how times have changed in 50 years), Chicago quarterback Sid Luckman was asked what he thought of the day's matchup. "We'll beat them and beat them badly," Luckman said. Privately, Bear coach George Halas

George McAfee gained just a few of Chicago's 381 rushing yards on this sweep.

thought his T formation backfield, which had sputtered in the first meeting, was polished to the point now where the Redskins wouldn't be able to defend against it. The polish was provided by Clark Shaughnessy, the famous Stanford coach, who helped the Bears perfect the T late that season as a favor to Halas.

The Redskins, though, brimmed with confidence entering the game, which was a historic one for another reason. A national radio audience was about to hear a football game for the first time, with Red Barber calling the play-by-play high above the field. When Washington owner George Preston Marshall took his seat behind the Redskin bench to polite applause from the crowd of about 36,000, he waved politely and confidently, much as a politician might. Then he lifted one of the songsheets he had distributed to the crowd to tell them: O.K., it's time for the pregame song. (Marshall believed strongly in all the pomp associated with the game.) And so he led the crowd in song.

"Who's afraid of the Chicago Bears, Chicago Bears, Chicago Bears,

"Who's afraid of the Chicago Bears, Chicago Bears, Chicago Bears, …"

And so on, until the crowd sensed there wasn't a voice in the house afraid of the Chicago Bears.

They should have been. Starting from their own eight, Luckman power-swept the Bears 92 yards in four plays, using the blocking and running force of the T, which allowed a pulling guard in addition to a blocking back to get in front of the ballcarrier. After a Redskin punt the Bears ground out 17 plays and another touchdown. After another Redskin punt, halfback Joe Maniaci sprinted around end and rushed 42 yards. After 13 minutes it was 21–0. After three quarters it was 54–0. In the middle of the fourth quarter, referee Red Friesel was nearing the bottom of his bag of allotted footballs. He had been given 12 for the game, and every time an extra point was tried, another ball went free to some spectator. So for the last two touchdowns, he told the Bears, "You're going to have to run or pass for the conversion. You can't kick it."

Marshall was embarrassed afterward. And angry. "Our defense looked like a roomful of maidens going after a mouse," he spat out. "Helpless, hopeless, hapless."

Perhaps. But it takes two to make a rout. And that day the Bears, battling for their first championship since 1933, might have played the closest thing to a perfect a game the league has ever seen.

This catch by Charley Malone was one of the few bright spots for the Redskins.

Greatest 17 Games

CHICAGO 23
NEW YORK 21

DECEMBER 17, 1933 The NFL was so excited by the 1932 unofficial championship game—the 9-0 Chicago victory over Portsmouth at Chicago Stadium 12 months earlier—that the 10 teams in the league were split into two divisions for the first time in 1933, and a real championship game was set. And what a game it was. "The greatest game I've ever seen," Red Grange, one of the stars of the show, said years later.

Maybe the weirdest, too.

On a misty, chilly day at Wrigley Field, Chicago led 6-0. New York led 7-6. Chicago led 9-7. New York led 14-9. Chicago led 16-14. New York led 21-16. Chicago won 23-21.

That's only part of the excitement of that day. The game is 60 years old now, and it happened in football's prehistoric days. But it was, at times, so wide open that it makes the run-and-shoot look like Woody Hayes football in comparison. In the third quarter, with the Giants up 14-9, Chicago quarterback Carl Brumbaugh handed to halfback George Corbett. In those days quarterbacks were eligible receivers. Brumbaugh went deep behind a surprised secondary and caught a 67-yard pass. Four plays later Bronko Nagurski took a handoff and surprised everyone by

Hewitt, among the last of the bareheaded breed, tossed to Karr for the game-winner.

throwing a halfback option pass to Billy Karr for the go-ahead touchdown. Chicago, 16–14.

The Giants had already done something never before seen in a game. Come to think of it, who has seen this since? Center Mel Hein later described the scene: "There was one man on my left, the end. All we did was have him take a step back, and the flanker on the right moved up into the line. Now I became an eligible receiver." Hein snapped the ball to quarterback Harry Newman, who surreptitiously handed it back to Hein; Newman began fumbling around in the backfield, feigning trying to pick up a football, while Hein wandered over to the side of the field, trying to hide the ball. The Giants used the play twice, actually, neither time breaking it for a big gain.

Anyway, at the Bear eight early in the fourth quarter, Newman handed off to halfback Ken Strong, who drove left toward the line behind a pulling guard. The Bears were ready to box Strong in, so he stopped, turned and threw a lateral pass to Newman. Then when Newman got boxed in and was looking for a way to get rid of the ball, he saw Strong waving his hands, open in the end zone. Newman threw a perfect pass to him, and the momentum made Strong tumble into the first base dugout, normally a space reserved for the members of the Chicago Cubs in a game played in far warmer weather. What an incredible touchdown! "If there has been a zanier play," said Grange later, "it probably wasn't allowed by the officials." The Giants now led 21–16.

It figures that the Bears would win on something freaky. From the Giants' 33-yard line Nagurski threw another halfback option pass, this one to receiver Bill Hewitt. About to get swarmed under, Hewitt tossed a lateral to Karr, who ran the last 19 yards for the game-winning score. (Today that's one of the most exciting plays in the game, the hook-and-lateral.)

Still the Giants had a chance for victory on the last play of the game. Newman connected with Dale Burnett at the Bears' 40. Grange, who would retire the following season, was the last man between streaking receiver Burnett and the goal line. Behind Burnett was Hein, trailing for a possible lateral. "I instinctively went for the ball," Grange said. "I tackled Dale high so he could not lateral."

"Grange saved the game," owner Tim Mara of the Giants said.

It was a game well worth saving, and savoring.

Greatest Games

CHICAGO 61
SAN FRANCISCO 20

DECEMBER 12, 1965 There were signs that something like this could happen, signs immediately evident in Gale Sayers's rookie season, 1965. In his first preseason game as a Chicago Bear, Sayers had a 77-yard punt return, a 93-yard kickoff return and threw a 25-yard touchdown pass. In his third NFL start he scored four touchdowns in a game at Minnesota. And then, on November 28, in front of a packed house at Yankee Stadium, Sayers humbled Tucker Frederickson of the Giants in a duel of the best young backs in football. Sayers rushed for 113 yards and two touchdowns that day, caught two passes and threw a left-handed touchdown pass that was negated because of a penalty in a 35–14 rout for the Bears.

All of this was enough to make Chicago's coach, the gruff and ancient George Halas, light up at the very mention of Sayers's name. Compare Sayers and Red Grange, George. "Grange wasn't so quick," Halas said, "but he had a fine ability to change direction, and he was a master of the limp leg—giving a tackler a leg and taking it away when he made his move. Sayers has wonderful speed, and he has tremendous acceleration and a variety of gears. He can lull you into thinking he is going at top speed,

and then turn it up another notch and be gone before you know it."

Two weeks after the game in New York, the San Francisco 49ers came to Chicago on a damp day to play the Bears at their Wrigley Field marsh. Ugly day. So ugly, in fact, that the equipment man was handing out shoes with long plastic cleats to the players in hopes that they would have better traction. In pregame warmups Sayers thought he could cut just fine with them.

In the first quarter Sayers caught a screen pass from quarterback Rudy Bukich at the Bear 16, darted inside to the left and ran the length of the field for an 80-yard touchdown reception.

In the second quarter Sayers burst around left end with a handoff, broke through 49er defensive back Kermit Alexander's tackle attempt and rushed 21 yards into the end zone.

Near halftime Sayers, his uniform now caked with mud, ran right this time, sprinting past linebacker Matt Hazeltine for a seven-yard touchdown run.

In the third quarter Sayers busted through the right side of the line, shook off tacklers and sprinted 50 yards for a touchdown.

Late in the third quarter Sayers

Sayers went airborne in the third quarter for touchdown No. 5.

90

leaped over a pile at the line of scrimmage, his entire body five feet off the ground, parallel to the earth. It was a one-yard touchdown dive.

In the fourth quarter Sayers shook off a 49er tackler at the Chicago 15, weaved this way and that, and probably ran about 130 yards. But it went down as an 85-yard return for a touchdown.

Six touchdowns! The total tied the NFL record, set by the Chicago Cardinals' Ernie Nevers in 1929 and tied by Cleveland's Dub Jones in 1951. It remains unbroken to this day. Sayers had 113 yards rushing, 89 receiving and 134 returning, a combined total of 336 yards, which still ranks as the fifth highest of all time. It might have been the greatest day a pro football player ever had. Who knows what might have happened if the field had been dry that day? And who knows what might have happened if the 49ers hadn't geared their entire defensive game plan that day to stopping Sayers? Said old Papa Bear Halas years later, "The amazing thing about that day was that Sayers scored touchdowns in just about every way you can on offense. He caught passes, he ran inside, he ran outside. He returned punts. I said it that day, and I still feel it. It was the greatest performance I've ever seen on a football field by one man." No one's arguing.

19

PITTSBURGH 35
DALLAS 31

JANUARY 21, 1979 "Terry Bradshaw couldn't spell *cat*," Dallas linebacker Hollywood Henderson said the week before the game, "if you spotted him the *C* and the *A*." Henderson went on to call Pittsburgh linebacker Jack Lambert "a toothless chimpanzee." And then he said the Steeler backup tight end, Randy Grossman, who would be blocking him during the game, "only plays when someone dies or breaks a leg."

But this game didn't need that kind of controversy. Supe 13 was already one of the most anticipated games in years, because it matched the no-doubt two best teams alive. The Steelers ran up an NFL-best 14–2 record in the regular season, then waltzed through two AFC playoff games by a combined score of 67–15. Dallas, the defending Super Bowl champs, had just crushed the Rams in Los Angeles 28–0 for the NFC title. But the Hollywood hype must have helped, because this game still holds a TV record that probably will never be broken. Of all the TV sets turned on during this game, 74% were tuned to NBC's telecast of the game. The 74 share hasn't been topped before or since.

We may never know about c-a-t, but we know Bradshaw can spell v-i-c-t-o-r-y.

Pardon the pun, but Bradshaw responded purrfectly. He converted two third-and-long situations on Pittsburgh's first series, then hit John Stallworth with a 28-yard touchdown strike. He linked up with Stallworth for a 75-yard score in the second quarter, and then, just before the half, he unexpectedly put the Steelers in position to score again with two long gainers to Lynn Swann. A rollout, off-balance seven-yard touchdown throw to Rocky Bleier with 26 seconds left in the half gave Pittsburgh a 21–14 lead.

But Dallas came right back, shutting down the Steelers on the first two Pittsburgh possessions of the second half. Late in the third quarter, at the Steeler 10, little-used 38-year-old veteran Jackie Smith, a tight end playing the last game of his career, entered the game. It was third down and three to go for the first down. The tying touchdown beckoned. Smith broke free at the line. He was stunned to be uncovered. He stood alone in the end zone when Roger Staubach spotted him and threw the pass, spiraling toward Smith about waist-high, just slightly behind him. "He was so open," Staubach said, "I could have punted it to him."

"I just dropped it," Smith said later, crushed. The drop haunts him to this day. Each year, in Hall of Fame balloting, Smith comes close to being elected but always falls short, despite the fact that he has far more receptions than either Mike Ditka or John Mackey, the two tight ends in the Hall. Smith thinks that his one unforgettable—and apparently unforgivable—drop is keeping him out.

A Smith touchdown would have tied the game at 21. Instead, a Rafael Septien field goal made it 21–17. Then, midway through the fourth quarter, an incredible outpouring of points began. The Steelers got 14 in 19 seconds, on a Franco Harris touchdown run and, after a fumbled kickoff, Bradshaw's fourth touchdown pass of the day, to Swann. Pittsburgh, 35–17. Dallas wouldn't die. Staubach took them 89 yards, finishing with a touchdown throw to Billy Joe DuPree, and after the Cowboys recovered the onside kick, Staubach threw a TD strike to Butch Johnson. Pittsburgh still led, shakily, 35–31. With 22 seconds left in regulation, Septien dribbled an onside kick. Bleier grabbed the ball. Jackie Smith clawed for it. Bleier held on. Pittsburgh won.

"Ask Thomas Henderson if I can spell now!" Bradshaw howled as the final seconds ticked off the clock. He believes, Terry. He believes.

Bleier's leaping grab in the end zone gave the Steelers a 21–14 lead at halftime.

Greatest Games

DENVER 23
CLEVELAND 20
(OVERTIME)

JANUARY 11, 1987 These were the obstacles in the path to Super Bowl XX that Denver quarterback John Elway faced on a gloomy and frigid afternoon in Cleveland several Januaries ago:

•The Broncos trailed in the AFC Championship Game 20–13.

•There was 5:32 left.

•On its two previous fourth-quarter possessions, Denver had moved nine and six yards. In the game Denver's only touchdown had come after a 37-yard drive set up by a Cleveland fumble.

•Elway was playing with a sprained ankle.

•The Broncos were getting Milk Bones thrown at them by the psychotic fans who dress up like dogs and form Cleveland's Dawg Pound low in the east end zone. Those things hurt.

•Last and most important: The ball was on the Denver 1½-yard line.

Grim scene for Denver. Delirious one for Cleveland, which had never been to a Super Bowl. The 79,915 fans in the old stadium on Lake Erie rained a deafening roar down onto the field, urging their defense to make just one more stand, and they would be off to Pasadena and the Big One. Elway walked into the Denver huddle just then, smiling. "If you work hard," he yelled above the din, "good things are going to happen."

Elway threw a five-yard dump off to running back Sammy Winder. A quick pitch to Winder got three more. Third-and-two, at the Denver 10. Winder plowed into the middle of the line, and Denver center Billy Bryan pushed nosetackle Bob Golic just far enough; Winder gained two. First down. Clock running. Winder again, off right tackle, for three. What were these fools doing, the fans in Colorado screamed at their TVs? Throw it! Elway tried to, on second down, but after eluding two near sacks, he scrambled for 11, to the Denver 26. Elway chose play action next, faking to Gerald Willhite into the line, and firing a strike to Steve Sewell, who gained 22. And then Elway found wideout Steve Watson for 12. First down, Cleveland 40, two-minute warning. Now anything was possible.

But Cleveland forced an incompletion on first down, and sub nosetackle Dave Puzzuoli sacked Elway on second down, respraining Elway's tender left ankle. Elway jumped up, hobbling. Third-and-18, 1:47 left. Then, disaster. Almost. On a shotgun snap, Watson was in motion between Bryan and Elway, and the ball deflected off Watson's buttocks. But it bounced

Elway's miracle-working skills produced another amazing comeback in the clutch.

to Elway, and he hit Mark Jackson for 20 yards, to the Cleveland 28. Unbelievable!

"Game of inches, huh?" Elway would say later.

No time for a huddle now. Elway threw one away because Watson was covered, and then he hit Sewell for 14 on a perfect screen pass. Then he threw incomplete, and then he scrambled for nine, to the Cleveland five. Third and one, 39 seconds left. The crowd pleaded with the Browns to stop Elway, somehow. Linebacker Chip Banks tried his best. He sprinted around end toward Elway, who threw low and hard for Jackson, in traffic, in the end zone. Jackson caught it. Tie score. Overtime. Elway had thrown, scrambled and generally harassed his team into one of the great clutch drives in football history: 98 yards on 14 plays with a trip to the Super Bowl on the line.

The end result seemed almost a foregone conclusion. Elway drove his team 60 yards on Denver's first possession in overtime. Then Rich Karlis trotted onto the field and calmly drilled a 33-yard field goal to win the game in sudden death. Was there ever any doubt?

"You know how you think, the night before a game, how you'd like to do great things in a game?" Elway said later. "Well, this is the kind of game you dream about."

PLAYERS

DON HUTSON

Sports quiz: What player dominated his era like no other in history?

Wayne Gretzky? Nope. Mario Lemieux came along. Wilt Chamberlain? Maybe. But lots of people consider Bill Russell the best center of their day. Babe Ruth? Well, maybe. Let's see how Ruth compared to the other sluggers of his time. In the 11 years from 1919 to 1929, Ruth won nine home run crowns and dominated the home run standings like no other baseball player before or since. The home run totals are as follows:

1. Babe Ruth, Yankees	496
2. Rogers Hornsby, Cards	258
3. Cy Williams, A's	211

In football it's tough to name a similarly dominant player, though Jim Brown of Cleveland set himself apart significantly from every back of the late '50s and early '60s, and Otto Graham drove the Browns to 10 straight championship games, a success rate unmatched by any other quarterback. But there is one other player, surprisingly little known to fans today, who recorded numbers even more impressive than did Brown or Graham. His name was Don Hutson, and between 1935 and '45 he made the No. 1 position in the annual receivers list his personal preserve. Here's how his receiving totals stack up against those of his contemporaries:

Player	Rec.	Yds.	TDs
1. Don Hutson, Green Bay	488	7,991	99
2. Jim Benton, Cleveland	190	3,309	33
3. Charles Malone, Wash.	126	1,801	11
4. Robert Masterson, Wash.	126	1,697	13

Imagine that: Hutson was almost three times as productive as any of his peers. No other player in football history can make that claim. To be sure, Hutson was helped by Green Bay coach Curly Lambeau's devotion to the pass, and by the fact that a good many talented players left the NFL during Hutson's career to serve in World War II. But if you're going to rank the 35 best players of all time, you're going to have to make some judgment calls. Naming Hutson to our top spot was one of them—we're sure it will start a lot of arguments.

Like Ruth, Hutson was a specialist in his league's home run ball—touchdown receptions—leading the NFL eight times in his 11 dominant seasons. In 1942 he caught 74 passes, more than four teams amassed in toto. In spite of the strong emphasis on wide-open passing since the '60s, Hutson's record of 99 career touchdown receptions stood for 44 years; Steve Largent finally broke it in 1989. Hutson played left end on defense in his early years, then defensive right halfback. On offense he often had to block tackles before going out on pass routes. Smooth, great hands, hard to tackle—Hutson could outfight defenders for the ball all over the field. And he was fast. In college, at Alabama, Hutson was an all-around jock. One spring day he left a baseball game he was playing, hustled to the track, ran a 9.8-second 100-yard dash, then returned to the baseball game. "He was the only man I ever saw who could feint in three directions at once," Eagle coach Greasy Neale said.

And he was great until the bitter end. In his last season, 1945, Hutson scored 29 points in the second quarter of a rout of Detroit; he finished the season with a league-high 47 catches. When the Pro Football Hall of Fame elected its inaugural class in 1963, Hutson was a charter member.

Hutson is still alive, in Southern California. A few years ago someone asked him how many catches a year he thought he might get today.

"Oh, probably about 50," he said.

"Fifty? That's not as many as in your prime," the questioner said.

"Well," said Hutson, "I am 74, you know."

JIM BROWN

Jim Brown had just turned 30 in 1966, and he was on the set of his second, and most memorable, movie, *The Dirty Dozen*. Filming on location in London, Brown abruptly and stunningly called a lunchtime press conference one day and announced his retirement from football.

Imagine the greatest player of his day retiring in his prime. Michael Jordan is 30. Barry Bonds is 29. Imagine one of them retiring, out of the blue. Imagine the shock people would feel. Imagine if Jordan or Bonds did it on a lunch break from his new job.

In one generation, times have certainly changed.

Brown retired at 30. Thirty! And coming off one of his finest seasons! Carries: 289. Yards rushing: 1,544. Yards per carry: 5.3. Touchdowns: 17. Awards: landslide Most Valuable Player award winner. Postseason: Three touchdowns in the Pro Bowl, in his last game, and voted the outstanding back in that game as well.

Just think what might have been. Another five or six seasons and he might have approached an unassailable total of 20,000 rushing yards for his career. He might have scored a similarly untouchable 150 touchdowns. But he has had no regrets over the years, and as much as football fans may have lamented his departure from the game, his years have been spent in a more admirable pursuit. Always concerned with the plight of African-Americans, he has spent his post-football years in the blighted inner cities of the U.S., attempting to break up the gangs and save the lives of young blacks who might otherwise ruin themselves senselessly in gang warfare. He has tried to empower blacks by bringing economic self-sufficiency to their communities. So the numbers he has built up over the years since football have signified the lives he has helped in our worst urban battlegrounds, certainly a more important accomplishment than building up 20,000 yards on our urban sporting playgrounds.

"I quit with regret but no sorrow," he said on *The Dirty Dozen* set almost three decades ago. "It's the right time to retire. You should get out on top. I've been able to do all the things I wanted to do, and now I want to devote my time to doing other things. I could have played longer. I wanted to play this year, but it was impossible."

Impossible?

"We're running behind schedule shooting here, for one thing. And I wanted more mental stimulation than I would have had playing football."

Rather than rehashing what might have been, we should be thankful that Brown gave us nine years, eight of which were spent as the leading rusher in the league. He never missed a game. His 6' 2", 230-pound brick of a body was rock-hard enough to ram through defensive lines and lithe and quick enough to pick his way through traffic on end sweeps. But over time he became most renowned for his jarring, crunching runs, his body like a battering ram with a football, a ram that couldn't be stopped. Linebacker Sam Huff wears a scar across his nose to this day from one collision with Brown in which Huff's helmet was driven down into his nose and a couple of his teeth were shattered. "I woke up on the trainer's table," Huff said.

Brown became the measuring stick for all the backs who followed him. Walter Payton couldn't run with Brown's power. Larry Csonka couldn't run with Brown's speed. Barry Sanders didn't have the same ability to run inside. They were all great backs—and still are, in Sanders's case—but the whole package made Brown the back for all reasons, all seasons.

OTTO GRAHAM

"Is the importance of football in the winning?" asks the general manager of the Giants, George Young. "Then how can anyone be better than Otto Graham? All he did was quarterback his team to the championship game 10 straight years."

Hmmm. Is that right? Let's see: four years with the brand-new Browns of the All-America Football Conference. Six years with the Browns immediately upon their moving to the NFL. Young is right: In each of his seasons Graham led the Browns to the championship game. And they won it all in seven of the 10 years.

Otto Graham and Paul Brown might have been the best football marriage ever. Graham, a bright and spunky quarterback from Northwestern with a better-than-average arm, was the first player signed by Paul Brown's new Cleveland Browns of the AAFC in 1946. Strange choice, too. Graham, a music major, fancied himself more a basketball player than a football star and more of a violin and French horn player than a big-game player. Furthermore, Graham had never played in the T formation that Brown would install with his new team. Still Brown liked what he saw when he scouted Graham and spoke with him. "Poise, ball-handling and leadership," Brown said. "Otto has the basic requirements of a T quarterback." Brown drove to the Graham home in the tidy Chicago suburb of Waukegan with a contract in his pocket, and he left, happily, with Graham's signature on it.

It turns out that Graham had the most important requirement of all. He won all the time. Starting in the AAFC, Graham took the Browns to a 47-4-3 record over four years, his crossing and sideline patterns keying an offense that relied on him and jumboback Marion Motley. When the Browns left for the NFL, there was a ton of pressure on Graham to deliver a winner. All the foot-ball people in the NFL thought Graham's gaudy numbers were inflated by the caliber of AAFC competition. A nice quarterback, they thought; let's see him against the best players in the world.

The first game in the NFL came against the Eagles, the defending champs. They had led the league in team defense in 1949, allowing just 11.2 points a game. Graham threw touchdown passes in the first, second and third quarters; he ran for one in the fourth. By the time the Eagles knew what hit them, the Browns led 21–3 and the game was in the fourth quarter. The final score: Cleveland 35, Philadelphia 10. That was one of the most significant games of Brown's illustrious career, because it showed that Brown—who had gotten such a fine reputation from coaching in the high schools and colleges of Ohio and then in the minor pro league, the AAFC—could beat one of the great NFL teams. In the NFL Championship Game that December, Graham threw four touchdown passes to lead the Browns over the Rams 30–28.

Graham threw for three touchdowns and ran for three in the Browns' next title win, in 1954 over Detroit. And Brown coaxed him out of retirement to bring the aging Browns one last championship, a 38–14 rout of the Rams in 1955.

It's interesting to hear people talk about the great quarterbacks in history. Graham's name comes up often, but usually after Unitas and Montana and maybe Staubach and Baugh—probably because people don't know what to make of the AAFC years. That would be like discounting Namath's year in the AFL. Graham was a .559 passer in the AAFC and a .557 passer in the NFL. His AAFC teams won 88.4% of their games, and his NFL Browns won 81.3% of theirs. Otto Graham deserves every ounce of respect that a Montana or a Unitas does, and a little more.

DICK BUTKUS

More than any player ever, Dick Butkus made defense a mentality. For years kids wanted to be Otto Graham or John Unitas or Ray Berry or Jim Brown. Then when this tremendous middle linebacker from Illinois burst into pro football with the Chicago Bears in 1965, the dreams of kids, and the game plans of NFL adults, changed. "I know what you're talking about," says Scott Berchtold, the p.r. director with the Buffalo Bills, who grew up in the late '60s. "A lot of kids stopped wanting to be offensive stars around that time. They wanted to be Dick Butkus."

Butkus never played for a championship team in his nine pro seasons, and you can't say he averaged X sacks a year to set all kinds of records for his day, because sacks weren't kept as a statistic until the '80s. (Unofficially, though, the Bears kept his sack totals. He had 18 in 1967, an exceptionally high total for a middle linebacker, along with an interception and a fumble recovery.) What you *can* say is that Butkus elevated the playing of linebacker to a violent art form when Lawrence Taylor was still in short pants. Butkus played middle linebacker like it was the nerve center of a defense, and he controlled every step the offense took with his sneering, domineering style of play. And his productivity was astonishing. In his nine seasons he was in on an average of 12.6 tackles a game. Today a player has had a terrific game if he gets 10 tackles. Butkus's average was 25% higher.

The stories about Butkus all make him sound so intense, so ferocious. When you see him on TV hawking stuff in such a neighborly way—yes, that was him on the late-night cable station doing a smiley infomercial for a charcoalless grill recently—you wonder: Could this guy really have been so mean?

The answer is yes. In 1969, after making a rib-cracking tackle of Detroit Lion tight end Charlie Sanders on one play, the 6'3", 245-pound Butkus poked his fingers through Sanders's face mask and into his eyes on another. After the game the Lions accused Butkus of starting three fights, and Detroit G.M. Russ Thomas called him "an annihilating S.O.B." Sanders called him "a maladjusted kid." In 1967 Butkus tackled St. Louis Cardinal running back Johnny Roland so hard he shattered Roland's face mask with his, giving Roland a puffy lip. Butkus was even accused of biting a referee during one on-field melee.

But he was more than a growling Bear. In 1970 the coaches of the 16 established NFL teams were asked to name five guys they would want if they were putting together a team for that season only. Butkus got nine votes, three more than any other player. He intimidated, yes, but he also read offenses as well as anyone in the game, something you wouldn't know from his reputation. "Nobody thinks I can talk, much less write my name," Butkus said in 1970. "I'm no freak. In the fifth grade I knew what I wanted to be—a pro football player. I worked hard at becoming one. I was fierce. I was tough. And they call me an animal."

What people forget is his football intelligence. You don't get 18 sacks rushing over center by being King Kong all the time. "At the key moment, the instant of the snap, I somehow know, most of the time, just how the play will develop. I stare—I don't know—right through the center and the quarterback. I watch for the keys, and they are very tiny keys, tiny little twitches of their shoulders or eyes. There's this split second where you put all the keys together and you know how it's going to go." And you knew where Butkus was going to go, but you couldn't stop him.

WALTER PAYTON

Walter Payton's body said he shouldn't be able to do what he did. At 5' 10" and 202 pounds, he should have been a slasher and a darter, a guy who made his living as a running back sprinting around the ends.

He did, kind of. But he also was a baby sledge-hammer, slamming into lines like a junior Jim Brown, and some people who saw both thought that Payton was better. Payton certainly was the most productive runner of all time, rushing for 16,726 yards and catching 492 passes, the most by a back until Roger Craig broke the record in 1991. But Payton played four more years than Brown, who retired in his prime.

There certainly has never been a back with the combination of speed, quickness, soft hands, work ethic and durability that Payton had. He missed one game in 13 years, and that was on a coach's decision, in his rookie season, 1975. Excluding his first and last seasons, when he wasn't the running hub of the Bear offense, he touched the ball an average of 24 times a game for 122 yards, combining rushing and receiving. He threw eight touchdown passes, one a 50-yard sidearm job while falling. In 10 of 13 seasons Payton rushed for at least 1,200 yards. He blocked like a pulling guard.

Through it all he was obsessed with health and with giving as much pain as he got. "My coach at Jackson State, Bob Hill, always said, 'If you're going to die, you should die hard. Never die easy,'" Payton said. "And that's how I ran." He willed away pain and injury. In April 1983, two days before arthroscopic surgery on both knees, Payton was playing full-court pickup basketball, something coach Mike Ditka couldn't quite believe. "He ran stiff-legged in 1983, and he still rushed for more than 1,400 yards. The doctor wondered how he did it on those knees."

Brown, who loved watching Payton run, knew. "He follows the code—the old gladiator code," Brown said.

How ironic it was that Payton's nickname was Sweetness. A better one, for sure, would have been Toughness. Said O.J. Simpson, "I broke my share of tackles, but I was never in his league." When Payton was asked how he wanted to break Brown's career rushing record, he said, "I want to go up the middle, hit one guy, bounce off, hit another and another, jump over someone and fight for the extra yard. I don't want to just break free around end and run unobstructed. I want it to be hard."

There will be arguments about backs until the end of football. Why is Payton the fifth player on this list? Why isn't O.J. Simpson higher? Or the Chicago meteor, Gale Sayers? It's simple. Payton treated every play like it was something sacred, and he did it for 13 years. It's like he was saying to the fans: Okay, I'm getting lots of money to play this game, and I'm on the field for 65 plays today. I owe it to you and my teammates and myself to play every play like it's the most important play of my life.

Which is why, when he was asked how he would like to be remembered as a player, he brought up sports' greatest hustler. "Pete Rose," he said. "Charlie Hustle. I'd like to be remembered as a guy like that, someone who stands for hard work and total effort. I want to do everything perfectly on the field: pass blocking, running a dummy route, carrying out a fake. All of it."

The ultimate hard-trying Bear, Mike Ditka, headed Payton's fan club. "It's possible nobody ever cut like Sayers," Ditka said. "And maybe nobody ever ran like Brown or slashed like O.J. But without a doubt, Walter is the most complete football player I've ever seen." End of argument.

JOHN UNITAS

A funny thing happened to John Unitas on the way to the real world. Football interrupted. Great football. Hall of Fame football.

There are unlikely careers, and then there is John Unitas's. A second-string quarterback at a Pittsburgh high school, Unitas got his big break in his junior year when the starter broke his ankle. After a nice but not spectacular career at the University of Louisville, Unitas was picked by the Steelers in round nine of the 1955 draft. One of four quarterbacks in camp, he threw more to the ballboys than to real players. After being ignominiously cut, he hitchhiked home from camp. He thought his career was over. And so Unitas stayed home that fall, playing for $6 a game for a semipro team in the Pittsburgh suburb of Bloomfield.

When one of the Baltimore quarterbacks, Gary Kerkorian, quit football to attend law school, the Colts' G.M. saw Unitas's name on the waiver heap, and he remembered a letter of recommendation that one of the Bloomfield Rams had written him about the kid. So he took a chance on him, and Unitas made the club as a backup. With the Rookie of the Year in 1955, quarterback George Shaw, at the Baltimore helm, Unitas's role seemed to be as an insurance policy only. But there was something about Unitas that the Baltimore coach, Weeb Ewbank, liked. A coolness. A calm. Here he was battling to make the Colts, and he never got rattled if he made a bad throw or a bad decision.

In October (Hollywood, you could have made a pile of dough on the John Unitas story), Shaw tore up his knee. Unitas would have to do. The rest is compelling history. With a better completion percentage (.556) than any rookie before him, he was starting to get a reputation. He would check all his receivers on their routes, hold the ball until the last possible second, never panic, usually read the defense right and throw the ball too accurately for some ninth-round pick off the scrap pile.

And he just kept doing it. No deep dark secrets and no gee-whiz stuff from Unitas. He was a quarterback, and this is what quarterbacks did. Throw, lead by example, play gritty, win. "There's nothing to get excited about," he once said. "If you know what you're doing, you just try your best to get the job done. If you do it, you're pleased. But if you fail, you can't let it bother you."

Unitas played for 18 years. He threw for 40,239 yards, which is still the third best in league history. He threw TD passes in 47 straight games, a record still standing. But two drives, as much as all of the numbers, put Unitas in these pages. They happened on the same afternoon, about 45 minutes apart in the 1958 NFL Championship Game at Yankee Stadium. The Colts and the Giants were in the midst of perhaps the most crucial game in NFL history. It was televised nationally, one of the first pro games ever on coast-to-coast TV. All the ad executives and New York money people were suddenly interested in this rising sport called pro football, and the game was terrific. With 1:56 to play, the Giants clung to a 17–14 lead and had the Colts hemmed in at their 14. Unitas threw incomplete. He threw incomplete again. Third-and-10. Then Unitas hit Lenny Moore for 11 and Ray Berry for 25 and Berry for 15 and Berry again for 22, with the crowd screaming and Giant defensive coach Vince Lombardi yelling himself into fits on the sidelines. Steve Myrha's 20-yard field goal sent the game into overtime, the first in NFL Championship Game history.

Unitas drove the Colts 80 yards to the championship the first time he touched the ball in overtime. If this was the greatest game ever, then Unitas made it that way.

JOE MONTANA

Where to start, where to start? How about with the death-defying comebacks? In 1975, Montana's Notre Dame team was losing to the Air Force 30–10 in the fourth quarter, and he engineered three touchdown drives in eight minutes. Irish win 31–30. They were down 34–12 to Houston in the Cotton Bowl in Montana's senior year—midway through the fourth quarter—and won 35–34, thanks to his two touchdown passes. And then there was the miracle drive and clutch pass to Dwight Clark to win the NFC Championship Game after the 1981 season. And then the 92-yard drive in the last three minutes of Super Bowl XXIII to come from behind against Cincinnati. And then the four second-half touchdown passes and 227 fourth-quarter passing yards, to bring the 49ers from way back at Philly in 1989. And then...

Uncle!

The numbers now. The numbing numbers. In San Francisco's last two Super Bowl postseason runs, he threw 19 touchdown passes and no interceptions. He is the alltime career leader in passing accuracy (.636) and has the highest quarterback rating (93.4). In 1987 he completed 22 passes in a row, a record.

The incredibly consistent greatness. He had major back surgery in 1986, and his most productive seasons came in 1987 and '89, his greatest professional drive in the Super Bowl after the '88 season. After a rookie year in 1979 when he was adjusting to the professional game, Montana never had a season's quaterback rating below 80 and never completed less than 59.9% of his throws.

In his first three full seasons his completion percentage was .635.

In his last three full seasons, not including an injury-plagued 1993, his completion percentage was .637.

He doesn't throw the ball as hard—not anymore, especially with the reconstructed right elbow—or as deeply or as beautifully as many of his NFL peers. But who has played better, over the long haul of an extended career, than Joe Montana? Graham was a more consistent winner—that's why we rated him just a little more highly—but for consistent excellence, Montana stands alone. Others may have played as well or better at points, but none have done it so well so consistently for so long. And his greatness in critical situations is just as wondrous. Whether it's because he's from the sporting hotbed of western Pennsylvania—the cradle of quarterbacks—or because he just grew up tough or because he received exceptional coaching or perhaps because of some combination of all of the above, he will surely go down as the greatest clutch performer in the star-studded history of the NFL.

"Maybe it's because ever since I was little I was involved in pressure situations plus winning traditions," he said in 1991, trying, somehow, to explain the unexplainable. "You knew you had to win, and you'd deal with it. What I want is the chance to play, to compete. When a coach would sit you down, when you knew you'd get yanked if you didn't do well ... well, that was real pressure. Once you know you can play no matter what, once you can get into your flow, then the pressure is only what you create for yourself."

His coach Bill Walsh once said that watching Montana drop back and get ready to throw was like watching football poetry. We're all the richer for having read Joe Montana.

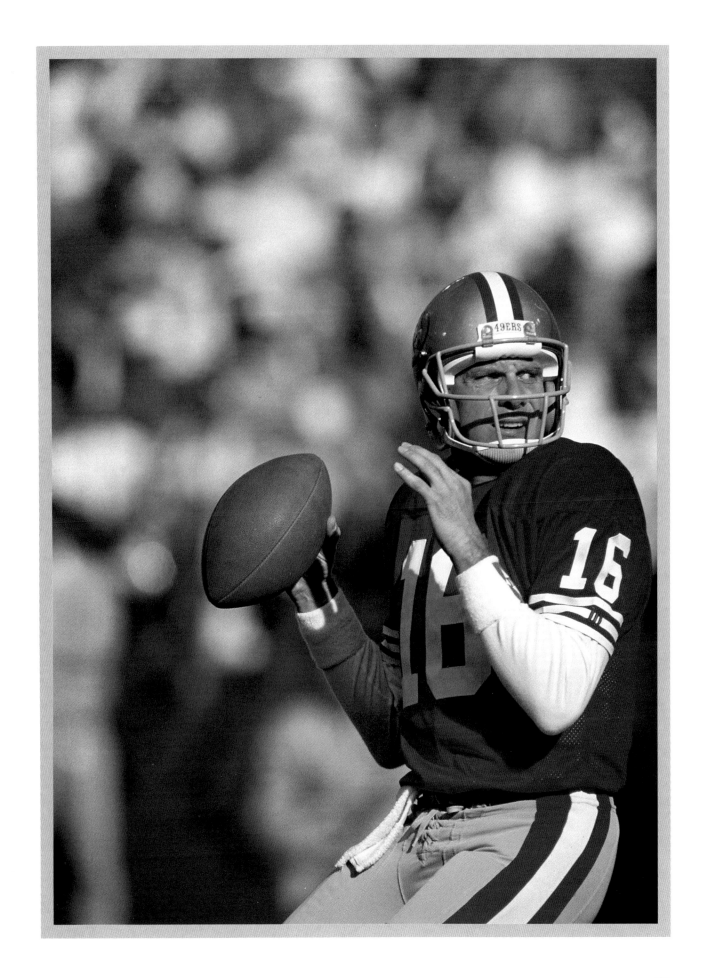

O.J. SIMPSON

The scary thing about O.J. Simpson's career is that we'll never know how great it could have been. We have an idea. He rushed for 2,003 yards in 1973, which has become a sort of Roger Maris–like number in football. It's an approachable number, but passable? Eric Dickerson did it in 1984—with the help of two more games and 47 more carries than Simpson was granted in '73. But Tony Dorsett and Walter Payton and Barry Sanders and Emmitt Smith and Thurman Thomas have all taken their best shots at it and come up short.

Anyway, back to the issue of Simpson's greatness. When the NFL was playing the 14-game schedule, Simpson had the greatest five-year stretch a runner ever had. He rushed for 7,699 yards in 70 games, about 110 yards a game. He never got seriously hurt. And you wondered: What about the first three years of his pro life, when Simpson was used as a runner, a decoy and a power back? ("If they try to make a power runner out of him," said college opponent Murray Warmath, the University of Minnesota coach, "it's like trying to put plumber's tools in the hands of a violinist.") What about gaining 697, 488 and 742 yards under those wise old Buffalo coaching owls John Rauch and Harvey Johnson? What about the fact that no one ever listened when Simpson, the Heisman Trophy winner in 1968, with the prettiest runs west of Gale Sayers, said in his early Buffalo years, "The more I carry the ball, the better I get"?

"Frankly," Simpson said in 1975, "I think my best years have been wasted. When I came to the pros I was 22 years old, I could run the 100 in 9.4, and I was at my best athletically."

Simpson may have left some of his greatness in a Buffalo locker room, but he had enough left to be one of the greatest players any of us has ever seen. The 2,003-yard year was his signature on the game.

It started in New England, with Simpson nursing a bruised rib that never was right all season. He rushed for 250 yards. "That's probably my alltime number one game," he recalled. In the fourth game of the year, Simpson was beating up on the Eagles, and Philadelphia coach Mike McCormack wrote on the blackboard at halftime: "TACKLE." Didn't work. Simpson ran for 171. In the last game, in a swirling snow at Shea Stadium, Simpson needed 61 yards to break Jim Brown's single-season record and 197 for 2,000. He got 200. He got 2,003.

On the Thursday before the record-breaking game the offensive line, which was one with Simpson for several seasons, met after practice to watch extra film. They didn't want to be the line that didn't get Simpson his 2,000 yards. At one point they all looked at each other and started chanting "We're not gonna be denied," over and over. And they weren't. And he wasn't.

Simpson's perfect season was a perfect illustration of what made him great. As he predicted, the more he got the ball, the better he became. He was a better player when he got tired. Some psychiatrist would have a field day with this one, but Simpson has a pretty logical explanation for it, and we'll buy it.

Early in a game, he says, a player's mind is overrun with game plan knowledge and scouting reports and assignments. He's thinking, not acting instinctively. "Eventually in a game," he once said, "I reach a point where I stop trying to outthink the defense and begin to react instinctively to the situation—to what a guy does, whether he can take a shoulder or head fake. I know instinctively what to expect. The more tired I get, the better I react. It's like a fighter who gets hurt and fights better because he's fighting instinctively." Whatever works, O.J. Whatever works.

SAMMY BAUGH

What distinguishes Sammy Baugh from some of the great quarterbacks who ever played is right there on page 324 of the *NFL Record and Fact Book*.

"Punting," it reads.

"Highest Average, Punting, Career (300 punts)

"45.10 Sammy Baugh, Washington 1937-52"

He led the NFL in passing three times as a tailback, throwing on the run most of the time, and three more times as a quarterback in his 16-year career. He was incredibly accurate for his day, or for any day. In 1945 he completed 70.3% of his passes, a higher single-season mark than even Joe Montana could accomplish. The record stood for almost four decades.

Another thing: He led the NFL in interceptions in 1943, with 11.

And one more thing: He drop-kicked better than any player ever, letting fly with surprise quick kicks from his tailback position.

"Sammy Baugh was the best player ever," said rival Sid Luckman of the Chicago Bears. "Nobody is ever going to equal him. Not anybody."

Think of what Baugh did in the best season any football player has ever had. In 1943 Baugh threw six touchdown passes in a 48–10 win over Brooklyn. He led the league in passing, with 1,754 yards and 23 touchdowns. He led the league with 11 interceptions. He led the league with a 45.9-yard punting average. In one season he was Dan Marino, Darrell Green and Rohn Stark, all rolled into one.

When Baugh began his career, it was legal for the defenders to hit the quarterback after he had released the ball, as long as the play was still running. Because Baugh weighed only 180 pounds, and because he was also one of the premier defensive backs of his day and consistently played on

every play of a game, it is amazing that he lasted longer as a player than anybody in the first 35 years of football. In fact, his 16 pro seasons were an NFL record until the early '60s.

In 1940 Baugh and the Redskins suffered the most humiliating loss in history, a 73–0 beating by the Bears in the NFL Championship Game in Washington. Two years later the 10–1 Redskins met the 11–0 Bears in the championship game again, foiling the Bears as they tried to become the second team ever to win three straight titles. Baugh threw for the winning touchdown in a 14–6 Washington win. He punted for a 52.5-yard average. He intercepted Luckman once. "Baugh was a headache with the unexpected," Bear coach George Halas said. "It is a principle that you should never kick against a strong wind if it can be avoided, yet Baugh quick-kicked several times on third down with the wind almost dead in his face. He tackled that wind like a sailor. That game was my disappointment of a lifetime."

At his size, of course, the startling thing was that Baugh never got seriously injured. Years later, back on his ranch in central Texas, Baugh talked about the beatings he had taken as a player and how both his shoulders sometimes had to be popped back into place and how his knees always ached and how he was always asked to play 60 minutes, no matter the game, no matter the score. Sometimes as a tailback he had to pick up defensive linemen and block them one-on-one. On the next play he would have to run, and on the next he would have to pass.

"When I went up against those big linemen, my shoulders would shake," he said. "But I never got seriously hurt in football. The only time I got hurt was when I got a broken rib from a young steer's horn."

BRONKO NAGURSKI

When the legend of Bronko Nagurski meets the man named Bronko Nagurski, we can't really be sure where the legend stops and the man begins. But we do know this: Even the verifiable version of Nagurski was one of the best professional football players ever.

For instance, there was the professional wrestling. He actually did wrestle for a long time, until age 52 in fact, and he even did it during his football seasons with the Chicago Bears. Nagurski simply felt that George Halas, the Bears' owner and coach, didn't pay him enough money for his many talents. "He tossed nickels around like they were manhole covers," Nagurski said in one of his many oft-repeated quotes. And the wrestling—during and outside the season, mind you—took the Bronk to all corners of the country. And it was real professional wrestling—you know the kind—where the wrestlers know who is going to win before they start. Nagurski was the Hulk Hogan of his day, and though he hated the phoniness and silliness of it all, he certainly could use the money.

Nagurski, at 6' 2" and 230 pounds, did most everything a man could do on the football field for the Bears from 1930 to '37, with a brief comeback in 1943 because the Bears were short-handed due to the war. He played defensive line and linebacker on defense. On offense he played running back and threw option passes frequently. He gained but 2,778 rushing yards in his nine seasons because Halas believed in fielding a large collection of running backs and using them all. "I was a straight downfield runner," he said once. "I wouldn't, or couldn't, dodge anybody. If somebody got in my way, I ran through them." Quarterback Sid Luckman recalls Nagurski as "a monster." Quite simply, he was bigger and stronger and more athletic than almost anyone else in the game.

And he was versatile too. In 1932 the owners of the best teams in pro football, Chicago and Portsmouth, agreed to a playoff game for the championship of the NFL. It was set for Wrigley Field in Chicago that December—until 19 inches of snow made the field unplayable. So they moved the game indoors, to Chicago Stadium. Prehistoric Arena Football, sort of. And in the fourth quarter, as the Bears were driving deep in Portsmouth turf, they just kept giving it to Nagurski. Three straight runs inside the 10 left the ball at the Portsmouth two, and Nagurski was handed the ball again. He sprinted toward the line, suddenly stopped, jumped and threw a short pass to Red Grange for the startling, game-winning touchdown. During the championship game the following season, Nagurski, perhaps the thickest man on the field that day, threw two halfback option passes for touchdowns in the 23–21 win over the New York Giants.

But the money just wasn't good enough in those days for a guy to play football forever. Nagurski had to go out and make a living, so he quit the game in 1937, only to return at Halas's request for the one season six years later. In Nagurski's last game ever, in 1943, he rumbled through the line for a three-yard touchdown, leaving bodies in his wake in the Chicago-Washington title game. The Bears won big, and Nagurski was gone, home to northern Minnesota.

The owner of the Detroit Lions, G.A. Richards, once told Nagurski that he was going to pay him $10,000 "to quit the game and get the hell out of the league. You're ruining my team." Nagurski made a lot of people feel that way.

LAWRENCE TAYLOR

There have been quite a few defensive players in football history who scared people, and there were a few who could shed blockers and chase the quarterback with a sprinter's speed and a few who had such tolerance for pain that the men around them were positive they would never miss a game—including some who would play so hurt that they actually scared their coaches—and there were a few whose glares could stop trucks. But there was only one who could do all of these things, and his name is Lawrence Taylor.

"He is the best player in football," John Madden said in 1984, in the midst of the Joe Montana, Dan Marino, Walter Payton and Anthony Munoz eras. And no one doubted him.

It's a shame that Lawrence Taylor didn't play 40 years ago. Not only would he have rewritten the book on playing outside linebacker in the NFL, as he did in his role as the league's sack king of the '80s, but he also could have played both ways—coach Bill Parcells used him as a tight end in one 1987 game—because he loved the game so much and because he was tireless. Absolutely tireless. And he hated to lose or be shown up, at anything. In a preseason game at Cleveland in 1988, he had been out for about a quarter when, late in the fourth quarter, the Browns were driving for an insurance touchdown against a team of mostly Giant backups. The Browns kept driving until they were inside the Giant 10 with less than two minutes remaining. Taylor grabbed his helmet and rushed by the coaches on the sidelines and into the game, saying nothing.

"Taylor!" defensive coordinator Bill Belichick screamed, trying to call him back.

Taylor reached the huddle, to the stunned looks of his teammates. He told Andy Headen, his understudy, to get out. "The man sent me in," Taylor said. Headen, grumbling because he knew Taylor was lying, slunk to the sidelines. "Right," Pepper Johnson chimed in. "LT, you the man."

On fourth-and-goal Taylor lined up at safety and at the snap of the ball sprinted toward center, where he collided with the ballcarrier and prevented the touchdown. The Giants held Cleveland. They still lost 17–13, but they held them nonetheless.

Asked after the game why he had run into a losing game completely cold—a preseason game no less—Taylor shrugged. "You don't let those things happen," he said. "Nobody's doing that to the New York Giants."

"But it's a preseason game," he was reminded.

"It *matters*!" Taylor said, his voice rising, his glare piercing.

Said longtime Washington Redskin line coach Joe Bugel, "The week of a Giants game, we used to have all kinds of special LT drills. We'd line up our fastest man, Darrell Green, across from the left tackle and force the left tackle to block Green as a pass rusher. He'd get exhausted. And we'd club the left tackle in the head, repeatedly. The speed and brutality, that's what it was like playing LT."

And that's the way he is. "We gotta go out there like a bunch of crazed dogs!" he yelled to his Giant teammates before a game once, a comment that the NFL Films microphones picked up. That sort of intensity became a Taylor signature. He played—and too often lived—like a crazed dog. But he overcame a well-publicized drug problem in the mid-'80s to play terrific if not totally dominant football in leading the Giants to their second Super Bowl ring at the end of the 1990 season. What Montana did at quarterback in the '80s, Taylor did at linebacker.

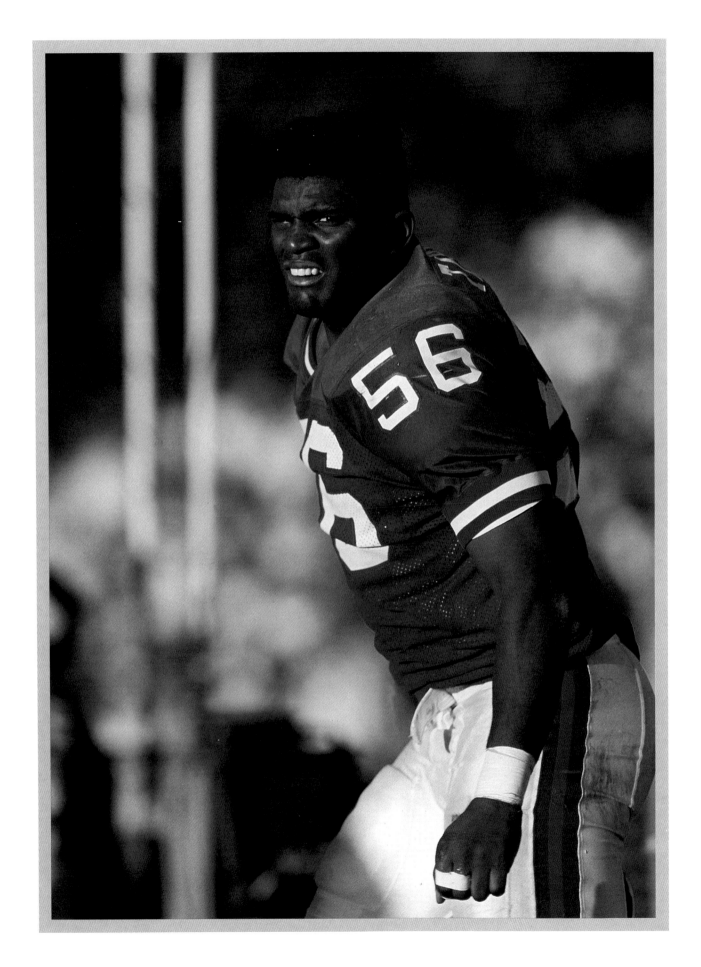

BOB LILLY

Once when the Dallas Cowboys were playing the Los Angeles Rams, Dallas assistant Ernie Stautner heard some strange stuff coming from the Los Angeles side of the ball while the Dallas defenders were on the field. "Lilly had those linemen so fouled up," Stautner said, "that I heard the center finally say to the guard, 'For god's sake, at least slow him up a little and give me a chance to get back and set up to try and block him.'"

That was the problem in trying to play against Bob Lilly. At 6'5" and a rock-solid 262 pounds, he was quick enough to play defensive end—which he did, at a Pro Bowl level, in his second NFL season before getting switched inside in his next season—and brutally strong enough to play a knifing defensive tackle. He played his way to 11 Pro Bowls in 14 professional seasons, and he made many of his most significant plays in the biggest games. In fact, that's one big reason why he appears so high on this list.

In Super Bowl VI, Lilly helped set a new tone for the Cowboys, who were developing the sort of reputation the Bills have today for winning lots of games but never the very important ones. After losing two straight NFL title games in the '60s and playing a very promising first decade without a championship, Dallas found itself up against a formidable Miami team just one season before its unforgettable perfect season. Lilly shot through a gap in the Miami offensive line, chased down quarterback Bob Griese like a German shepherd pursuing a kitten and sacked him for a 29-yard loss, the biggest loss on a sack in Super Bowl history. The Cowboys went on to a dominant 24–3 victory. "There's no use arguing with him when he gets hold of you," Griese said. "You fall wherever Lilly wants."

Long before that signature performance, in his rookie year of 1961, Lilly earned the respect of an entire league. It seems that everything back then related to Jim Brown, and this story is no different. Playing against Cleveland, Lilly and Brown collided with such force that when Brown staggered away, he walked toward the Dallas defensive huddle, not Cleveland's offensive one. "But I also remember a time," Lilly said years later, with his usual modesty, "when we met at the five-yard line, just him and me. Jim smashed in my face mask, ran right over me and scored a touchdown."

Well, let's do justice to both men by calling the Lilly-Brown matchup a draw. A man who coached against Lilly says he deserves to be in Brown's class of alltime greatness. "In my book," said George Allen, the former coach of the Redskins and the Rams, "Bob Lilly was the greatest defensive tackle ever. We tried everything against him, but we couldn't confuse him or contain him. He seemed indestructible."

Almost immediately after arriving in Dallas as the club's first draft choice ever, Lilly began playing with maximum impact. Coach Tom Landry moved him inside so he could play more instinctively and take advantage of his brute strength and surprising quickness. The one thing teams learned whenever they played against Dallas was this: If you're going to stop Lilly, you'd better keep a back behind to help block him; or else you'd better double-team him. "He was getting double-teamed 80 percent of the plays late in his career," said Stautner. That's almost a Lawrence Taylor kind of percentage. For an inside pass rusher to command that kind of respect and attention is extraordinary.

"A man like this comes along once in a generation," Landry said. "Nobody was better than Lilly."

JOE GREENE

Finally, in 1969, the Steelers did something right. The team had never won a league title, had not made the playoffs since 1947 and had suffered through five straight losing seasons. But with the hiring of Chuck Noll, a respected assistant from Don Shula's staff in Baltimore, the franchise seemed to be on the right track. Pittsburghers seemed to like the serious and quiet Noll, and they revered the owner of the team, Art Rooney. They would stick with the Steeler brain trust, such as it was, for another few seasons.

All that changed on draft day. Ignoring some questionable scouting reports from their own people (the worst: "I would question taking a boy like this in the first round as he could turn out to be a big dog"), the Steelers picked Joe Greene, a tall pass rusher from smallish North Texas State. The fans were stunned. Give us a quarterback! Give us a player to put our hopes in! Give us something other than this ... this ... unknown Greene guy. It didn't help matters that a contract holdout kept Greene out of camp until well into the summer, a development that didn't sit well with the veterans, who decided to beat Greene up a little bit when he got to camp. Or try to.

In the first practice Greene attended, center Ray Mansfield and guard Bruce Van Dyke, both starters, lined up across from him in a two-on-one drill. Greene's job was to get through them, anyway he could, to get to the quarterback. But Mansfield and Van Dyke had other plans, and they were going to be extra physical with the kid—heh, heh—when the whistle blew.

"The play starts," Mansfield recalled, "and Joe grabbed Bruce by the neck and me by the shoulder pads. We were gone, and it took him about half a second to get to the quarterback. We all just looked around and realized: Hey, we've got a player who's head and shoulders above everyone. It was like having a big brother around when the bullies were coming to fight you."

In 1969 Greene was a landslide defensive rookie of the year pick, and he got his first of 10 Pro Bowl selections. He was the league's most valuable defensive player in 1972 and 1974, and he and a brutal defensive core of guys like Jack Lambert, Jack Ham and Mel Blount lifted the Steelers to defensive dominance in the '70s. In the last nine games of 1976, for instance, this brick wall of defense allowed a total of just 28 points, and the Steelers went 9–0. Greene was one of those take-over-a-game-when-he-wants-to guys. In 1972 the Steelers stood 9–3 entering the last two games, and they needed two wins—including one against the Oilers—to clinch their first division title ever. In the game at Houston, Greene might have had the best game of his life, with a blocked field goal, a fumble recovery and five resounding sacks in the Steelers' 9–3 victory.

There is much more to the mean Joe Greene legend than we have time to list here, but one story of his intimidating nature must be told. Chicago was routing Pittsburgh 38–7 in Greene's rookie year, 1969, when, late in the game, Greene became enraged at Dick Butkus. It seems that Butkus was taking running starts at the Steeler line and just bashing the heck out of Mansfield, play after play, in an effort to get into the Steeler backfield. Greene, having had enough of this, burst onto the field, yelled some threats at Butkus, the meanest of them all, and then spit right in Butkus' face. For a split second Butkus thought about accepting the challenge but then chose to return to the Chicago huddle. Greene had stared down Butkus. He did a lot more than that to the rest of the NFL for 13 years.

CHUCK BEDNARIK

In 1960 Chuck Bednarik was, at 35 years old, the oldest man on the Philadelphia Eagles. He played full-time for the Eagles as a center and linebacker. Quite frankly his peers in the league thought Bednarik was a little strange.

"There's one big difference between Bednarik and me," Baltimore defensive lineman Artie Donovan said. "He's nuts."

That may be true, but at least Bednarik's nuttiness made him famous. Renowned for knocking Frank Gifford out cold in a 1960 game and for being the precurser to Dick Butkus in the NFL, Bednarik goes down in history for something much more significant: He was the last real two-way player—and a great one at that. There is an interesting story behind that accomplishment.

As an Eagle rookie in 1949, Bednarik didn't play anything. He was a second-string center, rarely saw action and never saw the defensive side of the field. But he switched to linebacker during the Eagles' training camp in 1950, and he made All-Pro at that position for seven years in a row. In 1955 he told coach Jim Trimble that he would be willing to play center and linebacker at the same time, but Trimble nixed the idea, saying he was too valuable on defense to risk tiring him out. In the late '50s, though, the Eagles had a hole they needed to fill at center, so they converted Bednarik back to being exclusively an offensive player—or so they thought. But in the fifth game of the 1960 season, at Cleveland, middle linebacker Bob Pellegrini got hurt on the first play of the game. With backup linebacker John Nocera already hurt, coach Buck Shaw turned to Bednarik and said, "Get in there, Chuck, but don't pull any hero stuff." He played both ways, and the Eagles beat the powerful Browns 31–29. He was solely a linebacker for the next two games, both Eagle wins, but when the Eagles trailed 10–0 to the mighty Giants at halftime in mid-November, Shaw told Bednarik that he wanted him to play offense too in the second half.

The Eagles went ahead 17–10, and Bednarik made the vicious but clean hit on Gifford late in the game on a crossing pattern, forcing a fumble and ensuring the Philly win. From then on Bednarik was a two-way player. In the championship game against Green Bay, he picked up a blitzer and flattened him, allowing Norm Van Brocklin to throw the go-ahead touchdown pass. With Philly protecting a 10–6 lead at their 26 and Green Bay facing a crucial third-and-two, Bednarik stopped Paul Hornung on a sweep for no gain, a hit so hard it forced the Packer star out of the game two plays later. And on the final play of the 17–13 victory, Bednarik bear-hugged Jim Taylor and tackled him at the Eagle nine, staying atop him until the clock ran down to zero.

The next summer Bednarik wrote a story for the *Saturday Evening Post*, and he urged other players to consider doing double duty.

"I'm not Superman," he wrote. "If I can play offense and defense, so can other professionals. Playing both ways is as much a mental strain as a physical strain. Once you think you can do it, you can. For a change of pace, how would you like to see Em Tunnell breaking clear into the secondary and Jimmy Brown charging up to make the tackle? I'm not saying that everyone could play both ways. I had a special reason. We were fighting for a championship, the first for Philadelphia in 11 years, and if I could help us win by playing both ways, it would be worth the effort."

For the record, Bednarik was a first-team All-Pro linebacker and an honorable mention All-Pro center in 1960. They really don't make them the way they used to.

JERRY RICE

You shake hands with Jerry Rice and, to yourself, you gasp.

"I've never shaken hands with a hand like that," you say to him.

And he says, "A lot of people say that."

They are big and thick and powerful and the longest hands you've ever felt, the kind of hands that can catch a basketball in midair and palm it, all in one motion. And certainly the kind that can catch footballs with the greatest of ease. He got these hands from working as a bricklayer with his dad, a mason in Mississippi. "I got used to hard work early," he said. "It made my hands rough, but it made me strong."

The best thing you can say about Jerry Rice, as it pertains to history, is that he should definitely move into the top 10 of this list before he quits. He has done to receiving numbers what Jim Brown did to rushing statistics. Entering the 1993 season Rice has already piled up 610 receptions. That's an average of 5.0 catches per game. The top three receivers of all time—Art Monk (4.5 receptions per game), Steve Largent (4.1) and Charlie Joiner (3.8)—can't touch him. He is 30 years old, has played eight seasons, and he already has the alltime touchdown record, with 103. Largent held the touchdown record, averaging a touchdown every 8.0 quarters. Rice scores once every 4.8 quarters. He shows absolutely no sign of slowing down, probably because he endures a Paytonesque off-season training program—it's a combination of the Parris Island and Carl Lewis methods—and still wants the ball as desperately every Sunday as he did when he began his pro career as a rookie out of tiny Mississippi Valley State in 1985. "Can't get the ball to Jerry enough," the incumbent 49er quarterback, Steve Young, says.

It's hard, of course, to make definitive comparisons between Rice and Don Hutson. The end of Hutson's career and the start of Rice's are 40 years apart. They both had great speed, although Rice's speed on the stopwatch has never been great. "Nobody outruns Jerry in a game, though," former teammate Ronnie Lott says. They both had terrific hands, and they both got open by hook or by crook, against any defense. We're just going to have to live with this reasoning if Rice, as expected, passes every receiver's record by the time he quits and catches more than 1,000 NFL passes: They're the two best receivers of all time. They played in vastly different times. Rate them the way you want. Our pick: We'll take Hutson—for now—with no slight to Rice intended. Hutson had Arnie Herber, football's third- or fourth-best quarterback of his day; Rice had Joe Montana, the best quarterback of his generation, and Young, at least once an MVP. And Hutson set records that no player could catch for years. With the way football's played today, you've got to figure someone will catch Rice sometime in the next couple of decades.

The highlights being ridiculously numerous—and so recent that you probably remember them all—let us leave you with one story of Rice as a kid. It might explain why, as Montana once said: "He just gets so ... so open." When he wanted to have some fun, he would go into the field near his home in rural Crawford, Mississippi, and chase the horses grazing there. The horses would run, and he would run. "They didn't come to you," Rice says. "If you wanted to ride, you chased them down." Rice would chase and chase. When he caught one, he rode it. Bareback.

Kind of like now, except he lets the cornerbacks wear equipment.

ROGER STAUBACH

Now here is something bizarre, just about as bizarre as Chuck Noll never winning coach of the year in the '70s: Roger Staubach never made All-Pro in the NFL. You can look it up. Four times he made all-NFC, but never all-NFL. Yet when he decided to retire after the 1979 season, he was the top-rated passer of all time. He had quarterbacked Dallas to four Super Bowls. He had brought the Cowboys back from behind in the fourth quarter to win 23 times in 11 seasons.

He also suffered 20 concussions.

Which is why Staubach decided to retire, even though he was coming off his best season ever. Staubach had career highs in completions, attempts, touchdown passes (27) and yards (3,586) in his last year, at the age of 37. And he hung them up in his prime as Jim Brown and Otto Graham and so many of the greats had before him. Now it's time to give him the due he deserves and put him among the best players ever, because he was one.

And like several of the great ones—Unitas, Montana, Rice—the road to the big time was a bumpy one. "I didn't play quarterback until my senior year in high school," he said late in his career. "Before that I was a defensive back and had spent one season injured. Rick Forzano, then an assistant at the Naval Academy, scouted me in my senior year and was interested. I'd never thought of the Navy before that. In fact, being Catholic, I'd have preferred Notre Dame, but they didn't show any interest." So he went to Navy and excelled, winning the 1963 Heisman Trophy. Even though he dislocated his shoulder in the College All-Star Game of 1964, he did enough against the Cleveland Browns to convince Dallas to make him their 10th-round draft choice in 1964. The Cowboys would have to wait until 1969 to allow Staubach to fulfill his mil-itary obligations, but big deal. What's a 10th-round pick worth anyway?

After four years away from football—one year spent as a supply officer in Vietnam—Staubach came to the Cowboys. It wasn't until his third year, 1971, that he got a chance to be a full-time starter. Eight years between starting calls. Could Staubach regain his touch, the touch that usually requires constant honing? "I had stayed in good shape in the Navy, playing a lot of basketball and a little tennis and football, and I'd done my best to keep abreast of the tactical changes in the game. So I was really no worse off than any rookie coming to the pros from college." At 29, playing for the first extended time as a pro, Staubach went 10–0, won NFL Player of the Year, and capped the season with Super Bowl MVP honors in a 24–3 win over Miami.

The next season was marred by shoulder surgery, but Staubach recovered enough to replace Craig Morton in a playoff match against San Francisco with the Cowboys trailing 28–13. Still down 28–16 with 1:18 to play, Staubach threw a 20-yard touchdown pass to Billy Parks, making the score 28–23. Dallas recovered the onside kick and Staubach took just three plays to win it, the clinching points coming on a 10-yard pass to Ron Sellers. And let's not forget the 50-yard playoff Hail Mary to beat Minnesota in 1975, and the two TD passes in the final 2:20 to snuff out the Redskins in his final regular-season game ever, in 1979.

Staubach's dad noticed something while watching Roger compete in a prep baseball game back in Cincinnati. "I used to dread the ball being hit to me when the game was tight," dad told son. "You seem to relish it."

Said Staubach, "He was right. I did relish it." We saw, we saw.

GINO MARCHETTI

When Gino Marchetti was growing up, the son of an Italian immigrant laborer, his dad used to warn him about the dangers of this rough game, football. "Whatever you do, Gino, stay out of the other boys' way, so they no hurt you," Ernest Marchetti would say.

Well, Marchetti went on to hurt quite a few people himself of course; he was one of the best defensive ends in the history of pro football, setting a standard for the position that few defensive players in history will ever touch. But how oddly prescient his dad's words were when the time came for Marchetti to make the biggest play of his life, and one of the biggest plays, it turns out, in NFL history.

It you accept the Baltimore–New York NFL title game of 1958 as the greatest game in pro football history—a debatable claim but one we support in these pages—then one of the most important plays of all time came in the 57th minute. The Giants faced a third-and-four at their own 40 and were clinging to a 17–14 lead. Frank Gifford took a handoff and lunged ahead, almost to the 45, until a brick wall named Marchetti wrestled him turfward, stopping him in his tracks. As Gifford fell, so did Baltimore defensive end Big Daddy Lipscomb, right onto the pile and also onto the leg of Marchetti. "Gino hit him first, and I plowed in to help," said Lipscomb. "And I fell on him." It sounded like a gunshot, a sickening gunshot. Marchetti's right ankle was broken badly, and he was in agony. But he had stopped Gifford, and in all the confusion caused by the injury, the ball got spotted just short of the 44, inches shy of the first down. Gifford was enraged, as were the Giants; they were certain he had made the first down. Marchetti's season was over, but he had made the play that allowed the

Colts to continue their championship march. After a Giant punt, Johnny Unitas drove the Colts to the tying field goal, and on their first possession in overtime the Colts rode another Unitas drive to the winning touchdown in the watershed 23–17 victory.

Marchetti stayed on the sidelines until overtime, then was carried into the locker room. "The docs were afraid the crowd might trample me if we scored," he said later. "I was stretched out on the table when I heard the guys coming in. I could tell they won. They were all whooping it up. Right then, the ankle stopped hurting."

Because of the injury, Marchetti was unable to play in that year's Pro Bowl, something he did every other year from 1955 to '65. The injury cost him the alltime record for Pro Bowl appearances. Marchetti was a ferocious and relentless presence—he played the run as well as anyone and could bat down passes with his long (6' 4", 245-pound) frame. He was also an absolute terror to opposing quarterbacks. "If they had kept sack totals in those days," says George Young, the Giants' general manager today and a former Colts assistant coach, "these guys today would still be chasing Gino. He's one of the most dominant defensive players ever to take the field."

"Marchetti was the best defensive lineman I ever coached against," said George Allen, who ran the Rams and the Redskins. "I don't think anybody who ever played the game was more difficult to contend with on the field. Then I coached Gino in the Pro Bowl once, and I can't forget how dedicated he was. A lot of good players don't devote themselves to the Pro Bowl, because they're hurt at the end of a long season. But Gino played the games like they were championship games." Most of the great ones do.

ANTHONY MUNOZ

When Anthony Munoz was coming out of USC in 1980, he visited team after team, all wanting to know if his surgically repaired knee was sound enough to allow him to play professional football. The Giants wanted him badly but flunked him on their physical. So did 13 other teams. That's right: Half of the teams in the league determined that Munoz was a medical risk not worth taking.

But when the Bengals scouted him, he contorted his knee every which way, he looked great on film and ... two visits took place that convinced the Bengals beyond all doubt. First there was a trip to the Rose Bowl where president and G.M. Paul Brown, son Mike, the assistant G.M., and son Pete, the player personnel director, scouted Munoz as his USC Trojans took on Ohio State. Munoz was a powerhouse all day long, making several key blocks, including the one that let Charles White score the winning touchdown. "The three of us sat there that day and just laughed out loud," Mike Brown said. "The guy was so big and so good, it was a joke." Second there was a visit by coach Forrest Gregg, who went to Los Angeles to personally work out Munoz. The upshot was that one old Hall of Fame tackle was thrown around by one future Hall of Fame tackle. Literally. Gregg asked Munoz to come at him hard, and Munoz knocked Gregg flat on his back. The Bengals were convinced.

How incredible it is, then, with this specter of injury hanging over Munoz, that 11 years later offensive line coach Jim McNally could show a visitor his offensive-line grading charts for the 1991 season, indicating that Munoz, then 33, had missed two pass-block assignments ... all season. "Anthony has to be the best lineman who ever played," McNally said, "and I don't see how anybody could think otherwise."

At 6'6" and 285 pounds, Munoz had the quickest feet of any left tackle in the game. He would have been All-Pro even if he didn't, because he was such a great run-blocker. The Bengals had so many different offensive styles during his prime—the power game of Gregg, featuring monsterback Pete Johnson, the quick-trap style of James Brooks under Sam Wyche, and the Brooks–Ickey Woods combination later under Wyche. Munoz could pull to the left for sweeps and roar straight ahead for the power game. As a pass blocker, his long arms and tremendous agility stopped every great rusher of the day cold. And his demeanor on the field was a role model's. Once he accidentally stuck his hands through Buffalo defensive end Bruce Smith's face mask. "He said the only two words he said all day," Smith recalled later. "'I'm sorry.'"

Said longtime opponent Smith, "I've watched more film of Anthony in one week than I watch TV in a year, and what's amazing is he does everything right. There are no comparisons between him and other tackles."

"This is all pretty amazing," Munoz said late in his career, referring to the high praise. He played 13 years with Cincinnati, making the Pro Bowl a league record–tying 11 times before retiring from the Bengals after the 1992 season. Even with a bum shoulder, he tried a comeback with Tampa Bay in 1993, when the money from free agency blew salaries sky-high. The Bucs and old coach Wyche figured: This is the best tackle ever. Even with a bad shoulder, we should be able to get a terrific year out of him. "I had no real desire to play pro football until late in my career at USC, and then I go and have this outstanding career, according to all these people. Why would an offensive lineman get all this attention?" he asks. "I don't know why, but I use it as a motivator."

GALE SAYERS

You had to see Gale Sayers to believe him. If you saw him in his rookie year, 1965, you had to think: This is the man who will be the greatest player of all time. He stood 6'1" and weighed 200 chiseled pounds. His thighs looked as big and strong as Jim Brown's and he had heavily muscled arms and shoulders and a tiny waist. With incredibly quick feet, sprinter's speed, a fullback's power and soft hands, who could imagine a record this man wouldn't break?

In his first NFL preseason game Sayers scored on a 77-yard punt return, a 93-yard kickoff return and a 25-yard reception. He scored four touchdowns in his third pro start. In his 11th start he scored six—on a screen pass, two end sweeps, a smash over right guard, a dive over the top and an 85-yard zigzagging punt return that left an entire stadium aghast; he must have run 135 yards on that play alone. It was muddy that day at Wrigley Field, and the players had to wear long cleats for extra traction, yet Sayers still managed to muddle through the mess for a combined 336 yards, still the fifth-highest total of all time. (One of the four ahead of him is the 339-yard total he would establish the following year against Minnesota.) His coach George Halas called it the greatest performance by a player he had ever seen, a pretty impressive tribute given the fact that Halas had been watching professional football games since 1919.

Today Barry Sanders runs just as elusively, if not as powerfully, and the two backs have much in common. ("He's the only back I'd pay to see play," Sayers says.) Among other things, and like so many of the greats, they share a near total ignorance about how they do what they do so well. Sanders doesn't have a clue. Neither did Sayers, who had an almost charming naiveté

about how he executed the moves that so astonished observers all around the league.

"I have no idea what I do," he said in 1965, after a game in which he actually pulled up near the line of scrimmage with the ball, faked a pass and blew by the defense for a long gain. "I hear people talk about dead leg, shake, change of pace and all that, but I do things without thinking about them. Like on the long run, when I faked the pass. That is not part of the play. The play was called purely as a run, but for some reason I faked the pass, and it worked out pretty well."

Sayers's 1965 season might be the best football season a runner has ever had. First of all, keep in mind that his statistics were accumulated in essentially 12 games, since he barely played in the first two contests of the season while getting acclimated to football after a summer injury. Nevertheless he scored 22 touchdowns, more than anyone ever had in NFL history; he returned kickoffs for a 31.4-yard average, a club record which he broke in 1967 with a 37.7 average; and he returned punts for a 14.9-yard average. His six touchdowns in a single game has never been exceeded. His 2,272 combined yards were the most a rookie had ever amassed in pro football history.

Two serious knee injuries ended his career in 1971, and his seven seasons were all too few for a talent such as his. Who knows? A generation later, with better medicine and more sophisticated rehabilitation techniques, we might have seen a 10- or 12-year career from Sayers, and maybe we could have fully appreciated him in the manner that people appreciate Jim Brown and Walter Payton today. Rightfully, after those seven years, he went into the Pro Football Hall of Fame on the first ballot. It would have been criminal to make him wait.

JACK LAMBERT

In 1973, when the Pittsburgh Steelers' scouts studied a skinny linebacker from Kent State named Jack Lambert, they kept coming back with great reports on the kid. But at 215 pounds? Art Rooney Jr., the scouting director, had to go and see the kid for himself. As it happened, it wasn't a game that won Rooney over. It was a practice. A supposedly light and easy walk-through practice was taking place for some inexplicable reason on a pea-gravel lot on the Kent State campus. Well, here was Lambert, diving to make plays. Diving, in a walk-through practice, on gravel no less. "He'd get up picking the cinders out of his leg, like he didn't even care," Rooney said. "I was shocked." And Rooney came back and informed the rest of the top Steeler honchos that Lambert was the real thing.

After a couple of years of greatness as a Steeler, Lambert was called by one of the Pittsburgh sportswriters "the Nureyev of linebackers." He said he didn't know if that was a compliment or an insult. He said he would rather be known as a Nagurski or a Blood or some throwback kind of guy. "That's what I really would have liked," he said. "To play back in those days even though the money was hardly there. They played for the game—and to hit. Cripes, 50 bucks a game, but they loved it."

Lambert, the Steelers' second-round draft pick in 1974, loved it too. With two front teeth missing from the football wars, he looked like the throwback guys he emulated, setting the tone for the Steelers as much as any player on that dominant, near-dynasty team. The Steelers were intimidating. They spit and slobbered and tried to kill you, and they played perhaps the most overwhelming team defense of all time—certainly the best most of us will ever see. "Jack took

us to greatness," beloved owner Art Rooney Sr. once said.

It seems almost unbelievable that a 215-pound linebacker should have been so highly regarded—he actually reported to his first training camp at 202—but Lambert didn't leave room for doubters very long. He started at middle linebacker on a Super Bowl winner in his premier season and was named Defensive Rookie of the Year. The following season, in Super Bowl X, he proved his mettle for good. The game was tight, and Pittsburgh kicker Roy Gerela missed a field goal, prompting Dallas safety Cliff Harris to clap Gerela on the helmet and sarcastically tell him, "Nice going!"

"Well," Lambert said, picking up the story, "we were getting intimidated there in the first half, and, I mean, *we're* supposed to be the intimidators. We couldn't have that. So I just grabbed Harris by the pads and flung him down." What startled the people who saw it was that Lambert actually picked Harris up off the ground with his hands and tossed him through the air to the ground. That would have made 15 tackles on the day, if it had counted—as it was he led everyone else, with seven tackles and seven assists. The Steelers won the game, of course, 21–17.

Lambert is a quiet man, a bird-watcher and family guy who now lives in a house he built from the ground up on 85 acres an hour north of Pittsburgh. He's a Pennsylvania game warden. But he had the persona on the football field of a Butkus/Taylor type who would never give in and who would always try to win the battle of the mind with the guy across the line. "It's like the old Greek drama," Rooney Jr. said late in Lambert's career, "where they'd wear masks, and eventually the mask becomes the face. Jack now thinks he's John Wayne." If the mask fits. ...

FORREST GREGG

Vince Lombardi always said Forrest Gregg was the best football player he ever coached, and if Vince Lombardi said that, it's good enough for us. Chalk up Forrest Gregg, right here, in the middle of our list of the greatest players who ever lived.

Lombardi loved Gregg because he was a team player, one who never complained and was always willing to change positions without even a grimace if it helped the other guys in the locker room. But Lombardi also loved him—and this may be the most important reason of all—because he kept the ferocious pass rushers of his era off Bart Starr's back.

In his 1963 book, *Run to Daylight*, there is a classic passage of Lombardi on Gregg, and it says everything you need to know about Gregg's skill and ability and unselfishness. Here it is, abridged just a bit:

"This is another real football player, this Forrest Gregg. He's a big Texan, 6'4" and 230 and out of Southern Methodist University, and I'll never forget what he did for us last year. He was as responsible as any of them for our success, because when Jerry Kramer's leg was broken in midseason, I had to move Forrest, my All-Pro offensive tackle, in at guard. He had played it one season, four years before, but he had to relearn those assigments, those pulling steps ... and he had to master again that knack of running at full speed, like a back, and finding that hole.

"He made no complaints, though, and he did an excellent job. My only regret is that it cost him a position on some of those newspaper all-pro teams.

" 'That's all right,' he said. 'I think winning the championship was payment enough.'

"That's the way he is, a team player who, if he has any selfish thoughts, puts them aside. He expects this of all the others too.... And he handles people like Gino Marchetti of Baltimore, Jim Houston of Cleveland and Lamar Lundy of Los Angeles, who are some of the best defensive ends in this league. He's a fine downfield blocker too. His speed isn't great, but he's very quick off that ball and he has the mental sharpness to adjust quickly to sudden situations. He has that knack of getting in front of the runner and, with his excellent sense of timing, of making the key block. When you combine all this in an offensive tackle with his ability and willingness to play guard, you've got quite a man."

For eight straight years his peers agreed, making him a perennial All-Pro selection, and Lombardi so trusted his judgment that he would change game plans if Gregg felt strongly about something. In the 23–12 win over Cleveland for the 1965 NFL championship, Gregg went to Lombardi and quarterback Bart Starr at halftime. Green Bay led precariously, 13–12. "I felt we could get Paul Hornung and Jim Taylor free on the inside to run because we could handle their men." In the third quarter, following Gregg's advice, Hornung and Taylor chewed up the middle of the Cleveland defense as the Packers put together an 11-play, 90-yard scoring drive that gave Green Bay a 20–12 lead and control of the game. His influence was no less significant in the Packers' triumphs that followed, including victories in the first two Super Bowls of all time. It is no oversight that Gregg is the only offensive player—Ray Nitschke is our choice on the defensive side of the ball—to appear on our list from the dominant team of the '60s.

"He's the greatest," Lombardi said, motioning to Gregg after the game. Who are we to argue?

RED GRANGE

Red Grange played his best football in college. On an October day on his Illinois campus in 1924, the Illini took on a Michigan team riding a 20-game unbeaten string. He scored touchdowns on runs of 95, 67, 54 and 44 yards—in the first quarter!—and later ran for another and passed for a sixth as Illinois won 39–14. A year later Grange rushed for 363 yards in a 24–2 win at Pennsylvania.

C.C. (Cash and Carry) Pyle, a theater owner from Champaign, Ill., came up with an idea for the most famous football player in America. The college game in the '20s was a huge sport, while pro football was regarded as tawdry, a game for tank towns and small cities. He told Grange he could make him $100,000 if he would sign a pro contract after the college season and go on tour with a professional team. Pyle got the Chicago Bears' management interested, and Grange signed with the Bears a day after his final game, at Ohio State in 1925. Pyle worked out a grueling schedule after the Bears' season ended—the Bears would play 19 games in 66 days, from coast to coast, including an incredible eight games in one 12-day period. The novel arrangement would pay Grange 30% of gross receipts, Pyle 20% and the Bears 50%. With endorsements (for a soft drink, sportswear, shoes, a doll, peanuts, a candy bar and tobacco), Grange made more than $100,000, though no one today knows the exact figure. His star was as high in the sporting sky as Buth Ruth's and Jack Dempsey's.

George Halas later described the signing of Grange, and the ensuing tour, as "comparable to the national televising of games" in making pro football America's game. The tour itself was remarkable. "The 66 days that made pro football," *Sports Illustrated* called it years later. After a couple of regular-season wins at Cubs Park (Wrigley Field today), the Bears took off with their Galloping Ghost, in a most amazing 12 days. They played a team of mostly morticians in St. Louis on Wednesday, December 2; Grange scored four touchdowns in a 39–6 Bear win. In Philadelphia in a rainstorm on the fifth, Grange scored twice to beat the Frankford Yellow Jackets, 14–7. The next day at the Polo Grounds the biggest crowd in pro history (73,000) watched Grange return an interception 35 yards for a touchdown in a 19–7 win over the Giants. Two days later, in Washington, Grange met President Calvin Coolidge in the morning and dropkicked a PAT in the afternoon; the Bears won 19–0. The next day, in Boston, the Providence Steam Rollers held Grange in check in a 9–6 Providence win. And the next day, in Pittsburgh, Grange, exhausted by the torrid pace of the trip, tore a muscle in his arm and played only 10 plays. Who wouldn't be tired? After five games in six days? With everyone on the other side gunning for him, trying to punish the great Grange?

Detroit and Miami and Tampa and Jacksonville and New Orleans and Los Angeles (with 75,000 at the Coliseum) and San Diego and Portland and Seattle also saw Grange. Everywhere he went he gave fans a reason to come see the professional game, and they must have liked what they saw. They kept coming back.

Two postscripts, lest you think Grange's worth ended right there: He caught the winning pass in the 1932 championship game, and he made the game-saving tackle on the last play of the 1933 championship game. The Bears won both titles.

"Pro ball in the early days got two or three inches on the third page," Grange said shortly before he died, in 1991. "After we made those tours, it was getting top headlines. We spread the NFL across the country." No, Red. You spread the NFL across the country.

TERRY BRADSHAW

Terry Bradshaw was lonely. Very lonely. So lonely he could cry. And he did. He cried the tears of a clown. His rookie year with the Steelers, 1970, when he was the first choice of the entire college draft, he would say all the right and funny things for the writers and try to be the life of the locker room and try to go out to practice and throw the ball a hundred miles on a rope, just to show everybody how much he belonged here in the big time, seeing as he'd come all the way from Louisiana Tech.

"There were nights," he said later, much later, "where I'd just sit home in my little lonely apartment out near the airport in Pittsburgh and just cry myself to sleep."

Ah, the big lug. But that's how it was with Bradshaw, who, more than anyone else on our list, experienced the highest highs and the lowest lows a football player can. When he got to the Steelers and he didn't play well, and he got benched several times in his first five seasons, he would sink into a pit of despair. Then when he would win a couple he would be the jolly guy in the locker room, puffing on the huge cigar given to him by the Pittsburgh owner, Art Rooney Sr. It was a roller-coaster, and Bradshaw didn't get off until, oh, probably around 1975. And to this day he doesn't think we ever saw the real Terry Bradshaw.

"The worst thing was, I lost my confidence," he says. "Totally. What's the worst thing that can happen to a writer? He gets a mental block. What's the worst thing that can happen to a quarterback? He loses his confidence. I was trying to be Joe Namath, instead of myself. To this day my biggest regret is I never threw the ball as well in the NFL as I did in college."

Don't be so hard on yourself, Terry. You were magnificent, after you worked the bugs out.

Bradshaw, despite jokes to the contrary (some of them self-deprecating), was the field general for the great Steeler dynasty of the '70s that went undefeated in its four Super Bowl appearances. He learned to play under the intense pressure of a make-no-mistakes coach, Chuck Noll, when the Steelers were primarily a running team. And then, when defensive juggernauts like the Steelers and the Raiders forced the NFL to liberalize its pass-blocking rules and prevent defensive backs from touching receivers after they'd run five yards past the line of scrimmage, Bradshaw's talents came to the fore. In the Super Bowl seasons of 1974 and '75, the Steelers rode Franco Harris's legs to victory and Bradshaw averaged 20 passes a game. In 1978 and '79 ("I was biting at the bit; I wanted to open it up," Bradshaw said), he averaged 26 passes a game. The percentage of total yards gained through the rush fell from 64% in 1976 to 42% in 1979.

During Bradshaw's tenure the Steelers won eight division titles and four world championships. He was great and he loved it when the game was on the line. He threw touchdown passes to win both title games with Oakland, in 1974 and '75. In Super Bowl IX he threw the clinching touchdown pass in a 16–6 win over Minnesota. In Super Bowl X he threw the winning touchdown pass to Lynn Swann in a 21–17 victory over Dallas. And he was the Most Valuable Player of the last two Super wins, throwing for 627 yards and six touchdowns, collectively, to beat the Cowboys and the Rams.

Because the quarterback is the nerve center of the team, the mark of a great one must be that he does the things needed to lead his team to victory and to championships. Bradshaw did those things, four times in six seasons.

JIM PARKER

A generation ago the Baltimore Colts would train in western Maryland every year, and one of the big questions of camp always was, "What does Parker weigh?" The weighty tackle always came to camp with some extra tonnage from his off-season hibernation, and he had an interesting way of shedding it. In a rubber suit designed for weight loss, Parker would climb into his big black Cadillac during the lunch period, the heat baking the Maryland hills a deep brown and causing steam to rise from the roads. He would roll up all the windows. He would turn the heat on high. And he would go for a drive on a highway outside town.

For an hour.

The floor of the car would be wet with sweat when he returned. His seat would be drenched. And when he would get out of the car and pull up his pants, the sweat would cascade out of them and gush onto the ground.

Ah, the battle of the bulge. Most offensive linemen fight it at some point during their careers. Jim Parker, all 6' 3" and 280 pounds of him, won it every year, and went on to become the first exclusively offensive lineman elected to the Pro Football Hall of Fame. Controlling his weight was hardly Parker's major claim to fame, though. That was largely based on the fact that Mother Hen Parker—his teammates also called him the Guardian and the Den Mother—protected Johnny Unitas so well for all those great Unitas seasons in Baltimore. Parker was drafted in 1957 out of Ohio State as an offensive and defensive tackle (he played both ways full-time for Woody Hayes). Coach Weeb Ewbank took a major gamble and moved him to full-time work at left tackle. Chancy move, because Woody Hayes ran a ground-hugging offense at Ohio

State, and Ewbank wanted Unitas to throw the ball 30 times a game. But Parker got used to it. He had to. In his first preseason game Parker played the whole game, and the Colts threw 47 passes. "We threw the ball more that day than we did my whole four years at Ohio State," he said. But he passed the test, because Unitas and the other Colt quarterbacks were still standing at the end of the game.

"It didn't take long for me to learn the one big rule with the Colts," Parker said. "Just keep 'em away from John. I remember coach Ewbank telling me my first summer in camp: 'You can be the most unpopular man on the team if the quarterback gets hurt.' How could I ever forget that?" Parker never did forget, not during that rookie season, not during the two consecutive championship seasons in 1958 and '59 and not through the many years of competitive football that followed.

Parker has a unique distinction. He's one of the best tackles, and also one of the best guards, ever. Midway through the 1962 season, injuries forced the Colts to switch Parker to left guard; he was on a four-year Pro Bowl streak at the time—surely such a switch would make it impossible for him to continue at such an outstanding level of play, wouldn't it? Not so with Parker. In 1962 he started another four-year Pro Bowl streak, this one at guard.

Parker was the first of the quick and mountainous offensive linemen who frustrated the great pass rushers of their day. "I used to think I could outmaneuver any big tackle, but that Parker can stay with anybody," New York Giants defensive end Andy Robustelli once said. That's why Parker is on this list, and why Canton opened its doors to him so quickly.

DAN MARINO

What Dan Marino is after 10 terrific professional seasons is this: one of the most productive quarterbacks who ever took the field—with no championships to his credit. If this book were to be written in three years or five years or maybe seven, who knows what number on this list might appear over Dan Marino's name. Fourteen? Eleven? Five? Three?

Well, let's just say what we know right now. He enters 1993 just turning 32, in his 11th year. We will hit you with some stats in a minute, but just know this, above all the numbers: One more average Marino year would put him in second place in history in every major statistical category for quarterbacks—completions, attempts, touchdowns, yards.

And with three more average years—just average, mind you—Dan Marino, at age 34, would own every quarterback record of substance.

He should approach 400 touchdown passes.

He should throw for 50,000 yards.

It's enough to make a figure filbert go nuts. When he was compiling the Dolphins' press guide in 1992, director of media relations Harvey Greene told his intern to disappear for a week and do the most extensive research on Marino's numbers ever done. The results filled 22½ pages. Some of the revelations: Fran Tarkenton needed 162 games to reach 30,000 passing yards, Joe Montana 147, Johnny Unitas 141 and Dan Fouts 131. Dan Marino needed 114. To get to 200 touchdown passes, Tarkenton needed 137 games, Unitas 121. Dan Marino needed 89. And our personal favorite: In his first ten years in the league Marino threw for at least 12,000 more yards than any of the current 18 Hall of Fame quarterbacks did in their first ten. Think about that one for a second.

"The stuff in there is not there for trivia," Greene says. "It's in there because it's so damn amazing."

Funny, but here's what makes Marino's chest swell with pride the most:

"The consecutive-game thing, I'm really proud of that," Marino says. Entering the 1993 season he had played 150 consecutive regular- and post-season games. His closest competitor: Jim Everett, with 85. "Lining up and playing every week—your teammates knowing you're going to be there. The rest of the records come from playing every week."

Maybe. They also come from the quickest release in NFL history, an incredibly precise deep arm. They come from Marino's uncanny ability to look at one, two, three receivers, and then maybe back at the first, and wait until the last split-megasecond, before he finally steps up and delivers the football. You don't complete 59.2% of your throws, career, by just stepping behind center every week and taking the hits and hurting like he must hurt. You just don't.

"He's a phenom," says Buffalo defensive end Bruce Smith, a good friend off the field, a hated competitor on. "There couldn't have been a better passer ever. I mean, the guy just doesn't miss. And he's not fast, but you can't catch him. Playing him twice a year is like playing DiMaggio all the time."

The shame of it all, of course, is that he could leave the game without ever winning the big one. Not his fault, of course. He hasn't choked in the big ones, or anything like that. He hasn't had the defense in the big ones. That's the trouble. It's quite a tribute to a modern offensive icon to say his only real fault has been he couldn't play defense too.

ALAN PAGE

You just had to love the class and clutch play of Alan Page, one of the best defensive players ever to chase NFL quarterbacks. In his 15 professional seasons he became the first defensive player ever to earn the league's Most Valuable Player award (in 1971), he earned NFC defensive MVP honors four times, he earned nine straight All-Pro awards, and he earned respect everywhere he went.

He had 173 sacks, about 12 a season. He blocked 28 punts or kicks, about two a season. He recovered 23 fumbles. He batted down 41 passes. He was the first front-seven player (linebacker or defensive lineman) who could play inside or outside, up or down, with equal skill and dominance, and he was the most important cog on the Minnesota team and its fearsome Purple People Eaters defense that allowed the Vikings to unseat the Packers and the Bears as the dominant team in the NFC Central. In fact, Minnesota was able to ride its defensive dominance, particularly that of Page and his three cohorts on the defensive line—Carl Eller, Jim Marshall and Gary Larsen—to four Super Bowls in the '70s. Alas, the team's anemic offense almost guaranteed that those visits would all result in losses.

Page could have played outside linebacker or defensive end, but his quickness and speed gave him an edge at defensive tackle that opposing teams constantly struggled to nullify. Many chose to run at him in hopes of neutralizing his remarkable speed of pursuit. Maybe the most amazing number in his career was 21½. That's how many sacks he recorded in 1976, which borders on the incredible, because defensive tackles are not normally big sack men. That total is also a full sack more than Lawrence Taylor's career single-season high.

And he saved his best, or near best, for last. At the age of 36, in the 12° chill of Soldier Field in December 1981, Page had 3½ sacks in his final NFL game. The Bears, his team since the Vikings unceremoniously dumped him in 1978, whipped Denver that day.

And when he retired, after spending nearly four seasons with the Bears (getting 40 sacks and 12 blocked kicks there, amazing numbers for a man with so gray a beard), he probably did the best job any player ever has of putting his career in perspective. "I tend to look at the broad picture instead of specific instances," Page said. "It's been more than a little bit fun, more than a little bit interesting, but I guess what I'm saying is that it hasn't been all that important. Football's just entertainment. Its importance in the world is blown out of proportion to what it really is."

Funny how the man could play so long, and so well, and apparently not truly love the game. "Football is an occupation in which you don't grow too much," he said. "That aspect of this business has always been a turnoff. You'd think you'd have to love what you're doing to play in the fashion that I have. But I don't love it. I've just always done the best I could."

A lawyer in the off-season, Page practiced in Minneapolis for several years, looking formal—indeed almost regal—in a dark suit with bow tie, his full beard flecked with gray. He became an assistant state attorney general in 1987. Then in 1992 he was voted a seat on the Minnesota Supreme Court by state voters, leading all vote-getters with 62% of the vote.

Finally Page was in his place, a place more comfortable to him than the football field. If he can be only half as good in a robe as he was in cleats, Minnesota will have a heck of a justice.

Greatest Players

MARION MOTLEY

Combine the mental toughness of Jackie Robinson with the physical skills of Ottis Anderson and Tom Rathman, and roll that into a 6' 1", 238-pound ball. The result would be Marion Motley.

One of the first black players in pro football, Motley was signed by the Cleveland Browns of the new All-America Football Conference in 1946, joining black defensive end Bill Willis. While becoming the top rusher (3,024 yards, 31 touchdowns) and best blocking back in the four-year history of the AAFC, Motley endured cut hands from purposefully placed cleats, uppercuts to the gut on the bottom of piles, racial taunts and unnecessary roughness, often not called because the officials, like 99% of the players, were white.

Philadelphia Eagle Steve Van Buren entered 1950 on a three-year streak of NFL rushing titles. That's when Marion Motley and the Browns entered the league and when Van Buren's streak ended. Motley gained a league-leading 810 yards, and the Browns stunned the league by winning the championship in their first NFL season. Motley hurt his knee in 1951 and was never the same player thereafter. It's sad that he never got his due in NFL history because Otto Graham was such a terrific quarterback and because Motley's greatness was fleeting because of the knee injury, and because Jim Brown came to the Browns so soon after Motley had gone. But there ought to be a place in this book for the preeminent back of his day—no cracks about the AAFC, because the Browns proved their greatness upon entry in the NFL in 1950—and so here he is. "Marion Motley," said Paul Brown, "was the most unselfish player I ever coached. All he cared about was whether we won or lost."

He played nine years in all, averaging 5.7 yards a carry (a half yard better than Brown, who played

nine years also) and distinguishing himself as maybe the best blocking back of alltime. By accident he also discovered the draw play. "Otto got such a hard pass rush once," said Brown, "that he handed the ball to Motley in desperation. The defense had overrun Motley in their desire to get to the quarterback, and Marion swept right through them for a big gain. In a short time it became Marion's most dangerous weapon." If Brown had used Motley more instead of building his attack around Graham, Motley could well be in the top five of this list.

"Inwardly, I always had the feeling I should have carried the ball more," he said years later. "But Paul Brown was a winner, and he didn't need any advice from me."

It was Motley's ability that allowed Brown to take the biggest coaching gamble of his life. In 1950 the Browns, in their first NFL game, drilled the defending champion Eagles 35–10. Afterward the Eagles groused about how the Browns had to pass so much to win the game, and they speculated loudly about how the Browns would do in a hand-to-hand-combat game. Well, Brown secretly planned an all-running game the next time they met, in December 1950, and it worked. Cleveland won again, 13–7. Graham threw no passes. You don't do stuff like that unless you're stupid, or unless you know you can back up your gambles. Paul Brown knew, and he knew because he had an agile Sherman tank in the backfield.

"The people who remember, who talk about Motley, remember the Motley who broke into the NFL when he was 30—on two bad knees," said Lou Saban, the old Denver and Buffalo coach. "He was just a shadow of the old Motley, even when he made All-Pro in 1950. I wish they could remember him from '46 or '47."

152

JIM THORPE

There is little rational evidence to put Jim Thorpe here. He was a better track athlete than football player. He hated to practice football, because he was so much better than the other players, and because he didn't take it very seriously. We don't know how many points he scored. We don't know how many interceptions he had. We don't know how many games all his teams won.

When an alltime NFL team was picked a generation ago, Thorpe was on it. His position: Legend. Really. That's about all you could call the guy, because he played wherever he wanted to play, and the records of those days are so spotty. But there is little question of his great value in NFL history. When the precurser to the NFL, the American Professional Football Association, was born in 1920, Jim Thorpe was named president, an office he held for the first year of the league's life. And he was a charter enshrinee to the Pro Football Hall of Fame in 1963.

Strange career. Much stranger life.

Thorpe, a Sac and Fox Indian, was born in a cabin in Oklahoma. A superb athlete in everything he tried, Thorpe made the U.S. Olympic team in 1912, at 24, and won the decathlon and pentathlon in Stockholm. "Sir," King Gustav of Sweden said to him during the medal ceremonies, "you are the greatest athlete in the world." Replied the nonplussed Thorpe, "Thanks, King." Of course, his Olympic career would end in tragedy when his gold medals were stripped from him by the IOC because of the semipro baseball he was discovered to have played in 1909 and '10.

When he came back to the United States he played college football for Carlisle (Pa.) Indian School, where he scored 25 touchdowns and 198 points and won the college football player of the year award. The next year he began his six-year major league baseball career, including stints with the New York Giants, the Cincinnati Reds and the Boston Braves, and he gradually became a baseball player in the spring and summer and football player in the fall. He played for the first dominant professional team, the Canton Bulldogs, in 1919 and 1920, moving to the Cleveland franchise in 1921 and then to a team he founded, the Oorang Indians in Marion, Ohio. The Indians were a completely Native American team, sponsored by the Oorang dog kennel, and they weren't very good. With a 1–10 record in 1923, the team was disbanded, and Thorpe finished the season with the Toledo Maroons. He played for four more NFL teams in the next five years and then retired.

Playing all over the field and boosting gates wherever he played, Thorpe led Canton to unofficial pro football championships in 1916, '17 and '19. At 6' 1" and 190 pounds, he was football's fastest player and its most bruising runner. He punted, and he placekicked and dropkicked field goals. On defense, he played the line and linebacker. With little protection and few pads, Thorpe was a pretty beaten man when he quit pro football in 1928 after playing for the Chicago Cardinals. But his accomplishments would live on. In 1950 the nation's sporting media voted Thorpe the best athlete in the first half of the century.

He's buried today in Jim Thorpe, Pa. It's one of the oddest stories in the history of death. When Thorpe died, in 1953, his third wife, against the wishes of his brothers and sisters, put his body on the market. Any town wishing some fame and possessing the necessary money could have the body. She finally found a town, Mauch Chunk, Pa., willing to change its name to Jim Thorpe, Pa., to get the body. That's where Jim Thorpe rests.

DICK (NIGHT TRAIN) LANE

What a long, strange trip it's been for Richard Lane, into these pages featuring the best football players of all time.

He played one season of football at Scottsbluff (Neb.) Junior College in the '40s and then four years as an offensive end with a military team while stationed at Fort Ord in California. When he left the armed services in 1952, he got a job in a California aircraft factory as something called a filer. I can handle this, Lane thought. An office job sounds great. "I was a filer, all right," he said with disdain years later. "I filed big sheets of metal into bins with oil dripping off the metal onto me." Disgusted with the job, he went out looking for work again and walked into the Los Angeles Rams' offices in the summer of 1952. They gave him a tryout, and in a scrimmage he made an improbable tackle while being knocked down on the play. "That's the kind of player I want," said the coach, Joe Stydahar. The Rams kept him for two years, and then he was dealt to the Cardinals, and then on to the Lions for the last six, and best, years of his 14-year career. He finished with no championship rings but with 68 interceptions, third in history behind Paul Krause and Emlen Tunnell.

In camp that year Lane started as a wide receiver, and often he would go to the room of star wideout Tom Fears, looking for advice. Fears was partial to the music of Buddy Morrow, and night after night Fears would play Morrow, often with Lane in the room. "Night Train" was Fears's favorite Morrow song, and teammate Ben Sheets saw Lane in the room when it was playing one night. "Hey, Night Train," Sheets said, christening Lane.

Well, the Rams switched the 6'2", 180-pound, cat-quick Lane to defensive cornerback that year, and all he did was intercept more balls than any player ever has in any NFL season, 14. Lane became a wily scientist at the position, often lecturing teammates in the art of pass defense. "Don't throw anywhere near him. He's the best there is," Vince Lombardi often reminded Bart Starr.

As quoted by writer George Plimpton, here is how the Night Train worked his magic:

"I set the fellow up by baiting him just a li'l bit, giving him just a bit to the outside on the zone coverage maybe, until this fellow goes back to his quarterback, and he tells him in the huddle, 'Lawd Almighty, I can beat Night Train to the outside, beat him like a drum,' and he *plead* with the quarterback to throw him the ball out there, he practically get down on his *knees* asking for the ball. The quarterback may have been around a long time, and maybe he smell a rat, especially when the talk is about Night Train's zone, but then he figure maybe there's no *harm* in trying a pass out there. So he says OK. He calls the play. I watch my man as he lines up. He's trying to look the same as he always does, but he don't—there's something about him, something I can read, trotting out and standing there at the flanker, maybe by the way he curls his fingers, maybe a bit too casual, maybe something you can't see, but just feel. Joe Schmidt, who calls the defensive signals, calls the blue coverage, which is what I hope he does, and where before I don' move, I'm there, and that boy, who runs out there looking to make the touchdown *easy*, why, he's like to be in bad trouble. Maybe a Night Train interception."

When Plimpton watched Lane in practice, he saw the offense throw two passes at his corner. One Lane knocked down. The other was caught by the receiver, causing Lane to start laughing. "It occurred to me that Night Train had such confidence that such a mistake could only be treated as ludicrous, and therefore comic," Plimpton wrote.

RAY NITSCHKE

First of all, Ray Nitschke looked the part. He came into the league without too much hair and sort of mean-looking; halfway through his career, around 1965, he was almost completely bald and downright ferocious-looking. But even more important, Nitschke played the part. The key to the best defense on one of football history's best teams, Nitschke, all 6'3" and 235 pounds of him, roamed the field and hit with abandon, sometimes yelling crazy things while tackling other players. Even his own teammates were terrified of him.

He was the starting middle linebacker and defensive signal-caller for the Packers in six NFL Championship Games and two Super Bowls. Green Bay went 7–1 in those games, the only loss coming in the very first title game against the Philadelphia Eagles in 1960. The opposition scored a paltry 13 points a game, on average, in those games. And in those eight games collectively Nitschke was the leading Packer tackler. Only once during those eight games was the MVP a defensive player—Nitschke, in the 16–7 whipping of the Giants in the 1962 championship game—and afterward Vince Lombardi said to his team, "Today you were the greatest team in the history of the National Football League. And I mean it." His teammates voted him the Most Valuable Packer in the championship year of 1967. And when the NFL's 50th anniversary team was named in 1972, Nitschke was one of the three linebackers selected.

Nitschke, though, had lots of maturing to do when he entered the league in 1958 as a third-round fullback-linebacker prospect from Illinois. By the time he was in high school both his parents had died, and he began to go through life seething with anger at the hand he had been dealt. Because Nitschke was in and out of trouble at Illinois, the Packers took a chance when they picked him so high in the draft. But Lombardi thought that if he could just harness that boundless aggression and anger, he would have himself a heck of a player. It wasn't easy. In 1959, frustrated at being on Lombardi's bench, he would shout in the locker room, "Just call me the judge. Call me the judge. 'Cause I'm always on the bench."

A full-time starter beginning in 1961, Nitschke began controlling games by sheer force of will, and the anger he had inside him was coming out at the opposition now. But Lombardi still treated him like a dog on a leash. According to *Vince: A Personal Biography of Vince Lombardi*, Lombardi would often scream on the practice field at the chattering, hyperactive Nitschke, "Hey, Nitschke! Shaddup!"

Later Nitschke said, "He helped me to turn around as a person. He inspired me by his determination in what he did."

And he always hated being called an animal, although that's how people think of guys like Nitschke and Butkus and Lambert, the great linebackers of our generation. "Linebackers, by the nature of their position, have to be aggressive. If you really love football, that's where you want to be," Nitschke said. "But you're not an animal. That's a sportscaster tag, and they say a lot of the wrong things."

Still, you've got to figure Lombardi got away with something pretty risky after the Packers beat the Cardinals 31–23 in 1967. So taken with the moment was Lombardi, and so taken with the brute-force play of Nitschke that day, that Lombardi went to Nitschke in the locker room and kissed him. Smack on the cheek. There was never much of that soft stuff around Ray Nitschke.

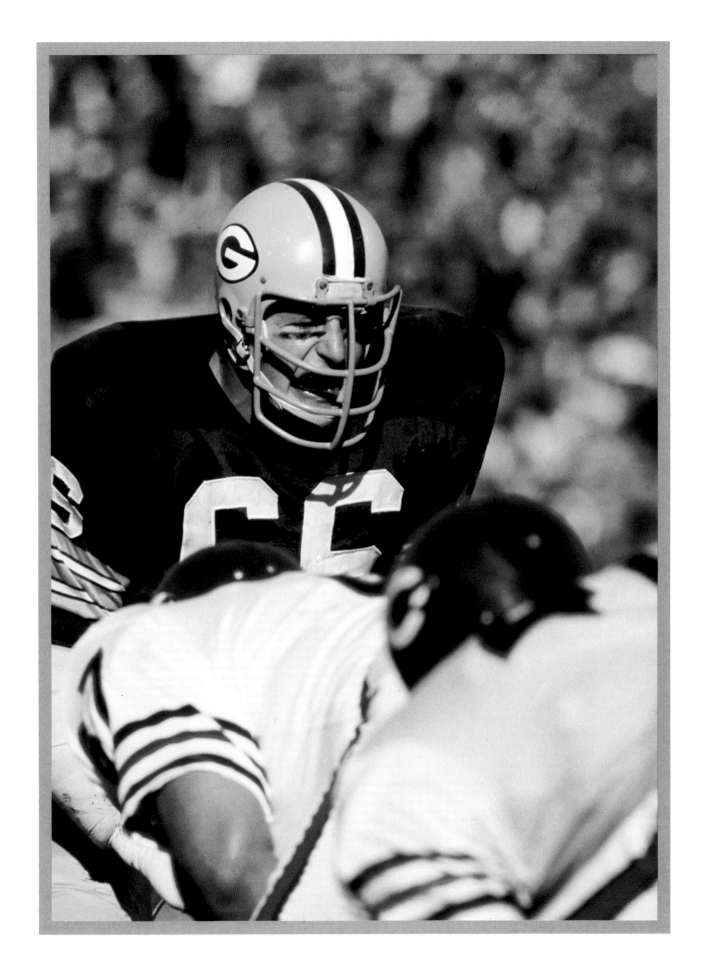

STEVE LARGENT

Nice guys finish 31st.

It could well be argued that after Don Hutson and Jerry Rice, the next-best receiver of all time is Raymond Berry, who was so clutch for the great Colt teams. Or maybe Art Monk, so graceful and reliable, or James Lofton, so smart and athletic, or Otto Graham's great receivers with the Browns, Dante Lavelli or Mac Speedie, or the durable Charlie Joiner. All are deserving. Steve Largent, one of the most admirable guys to ever don a uniform in any sport, is our pick.

In many ways Largent's success was simply the product of several systems designed to maximize passing, because the rest of the Seattle offense was often so talentless, and the product of an age in football where, on offense, anything went.

But his quarterbacks were Jim Zorn, who threw 26 more interceptions than touchdowns in his 11 NFL seasons, and Dave Krieg, the NFL's alltime leading fumbler. Largent was phenomenally healthy, missing only 10 nonstrike games in his 14 seasons due to injury; in his first 13 years he missed but four. And he faced some of the best defensive backs in NFL history twice a year in a division, the AFC West, that seemed to grow great cornerbacks and safeties. He faced three corners who will be considered for the Hall of Fame someday—Mike Haynes and Lester Hayes of the Raiders and Albert Lewis of Kansas City—and tough Gill Byrd of San Diego. He went up against Pro Bowl safeties like Dennis Smith of Denver and Deron Cherry of the Chiefs and, early in his career, Jack Tatum of the Raiders.

Through it all he set records for career receptions (819), receiving yards (13,089), 1,000-yard seasons (eight), touchdown receptions (100) and consecutive games with a reception (177). The marks for receptions, touchdowns and yardage are already broken; the others probably someday will be. Largent wasn't the greatest receiver who ever played—he was more like the Carl Yastrzemski of receivers. He was always there, always putting up solid numbers, year after year, on mostly mediocre teams. Seattle was 106–113 in Largent's career; only once did he make it as far as the AFC Championship Game.

An immensely popular player, Largent will always be known as one of the nicer guys in sports history. He took his regular neighborhood turn carpooling the kids to school each Monday, even during the football season. Late in his career his house, on Lake Washington in a Seattle suburb, was always filled with kids playing, often with Largent at the bottom of a pile. He volunteered for every charity he could. And what a practice player and team player. Find a teammate who didn't like Steve Largent, and you've found a teammate who didn't like apple pie.

"You're never as good or bad as they say you are," he said in a common moment of self-deprecation in 1986. "How significant or insignificant am I? In the context of eternity, my football achievements mean very little. To a large extent my job consists of running downfield, beating a guy and catching a ball. In one-on-one defense, anyone should be able to get open."

But Mike Haynes once said, "He's the most deceptive receiver in football. What makes him so special is that he'll change patterns to fit the situation. It's almost as if the quarterback says to him in the huddle, 'Do whatever you want. Just get yourself open, and I'll throw to you.'"

"Steve," said Lester Hayes, "is the master of tomfoolery. He has run pass routes on me that I've never seen or dreamed about." Join the club, Lester.

FRAN TARKENTON

There is this belief among professional football people that unless you won a championship, your career is somehow diminished in history. In fact, it is diminished—a lot. And it's diminished even further when you don't do things in a classic, by-the-book sort of way. These are the only possible explanations for Fran Tarkenton not making the Pro Football Hall of Fame until his third year of eligibility.

Despite being just six feet and 190 pounds, Tarkenton was one of the most durable quarterbacks in history, playing 18 years. He set records that have lived for 15 years, 15 years worth of longer seasons and more explosive offenses. Dan Marino should break them, but it's not a lock, not in this physical game. Tarkenton threw for almost 4,000 more yards (47,003) than No. 2 Dan Fouts, for 52 more touchdowns than No. 2 Johnny Unitas (342) and for more completions and attempts than anyone. Ever. Before Randall Cunningham broke the record in 1992, Tarkenton had rushed for more yards (3,674) than any quarterback ever, as well. In fact, it is unlikely that you would see as many running quarterbacks today were it not for the example set by Tarkenton, who proved that you could run an efficient offense and still improvise every once in a while.

Is it a great player's fault that he is on bad teams or on teams that don't win championships? Obviously, in this, the ultimate team sport, one player can lift a team only so much. The Oorang Indians went 1–10 with Jim Thorpe in 1922, the Pittsburgh Steelers 1–13 with Joe Greene in 1969, the San Francisco 49ers 6–10 with Joe Montana in 1980. Should Tarkenton be blamed because the defense-happy Vikings never surrounded him with the offensive players to complement his outstanding skills? According to the

numbers his teams were above average. His 18 Minnesota Viking and New York Giant teams went 131-117-6, pretty good considering his first starting job was with the expansion Vikings in 1961, and the Giants were coming off a 1-12-1 season when they traded for him in 1967. In the playoffs he went 7–5. He lost three Super Bowls. He won one NFL title, in 1969. And he missed nine games in 18 years because of coach's decisions or injury.

This is a loser?

Throughout his career he was a vibrant and enthusiastic player, running all over the field trying to make plays. Given his propensity to scramble, it's amazing he wasn't hurt more, but he hardly ever was. Luck of the quarterback draw, must be. In his first NFL game ever, which was also the Vikings' first, he came off the Minnesota bench to throw for four touchdowns and run for a fifth in a 37–13 upset of Chicago. In 1975 he scrambled for 28 seconds before finding Sammy White for a 45-yard touchdown. Is that a loser?

He never had the bitterness he might have had because of the way history had slighted him.

"I think Unitas was the best," Tarkenton said late in his career, when he was on his second tour of duty with the Vikings. "But he didn't see the zones and subtle defenses we see. He got a lot of one-on-one coverage. He didn't see the pass rush we see.

"I'd like to be thought of as a good one. I hate to think I won't be unless I win a Super Bowl. You know, this team could win a Super Bowl, but I don't know that I would have made a bigger contribution to football by being a part of it than I did a couple of seasons when we went 9–5 and 7–7 with no football players."

JOE NAMATH

Some athletes were born for the stage, for the great games, for the big events. It's not that they play poorly in other settings. It's that they feel most at home when there's a penalty shot to be scored, a winning three-pointer to be sunk at the buzzer, a Super Bowl to be won. "My kind of guy," says Jimmy Johnson, the coach of today's Cowboys, "is the guy who swaggers into the pool hall and says, 'Let me sink that eight ball.'"

Jimmy Johnson should have coached Joe Namath.

Namath threw 47 more interceptions than touchdowns, the biggest negative margin of any quarterback in the Pro Football Hall of Fame. His completion percentage was a relatively poor 50.1%. He was capable of great and awful things, even on consecutive plays. On October 15, 1967, he threw six interceptions in a game, which tied an AFL record. The next two weeks he threw 15 straight completions, which tied an AFL record. The same season he had the most prolific passing year in AFL history, throwing for 4,007 yards in just 14 games.

Just think how high his highs would have been without his four knee surgeries—he has two artificial knees today—and wrist and ankle injuries. The guy went into Baltimore in 1972, with the Colts coming off a playoff season and Namath coming off major surgery on his left knee in 1971, and threw for 496 yards and six touchdowns. Are there stats for guts and guile and savvy and nerve and playing in immense pain? Let's make a list of those guys for another pro football history book. Let's put Namath up there with the Jim Ottos and the Dan Hamptons and all the other uncomplaining football warriors.

Namath never namby-pambied his way through games or through his contacts with the media.

He never said the right things because they were politically correct. Just because everyone told him that the Baltimore Colts were 18-point favorites in Super Bowl III, why did he have to believe it? Why did he have to buy into the p.r. machine of the National Football League, the hype that said everything about the big and brassy NFL was better than everything about the "Little Engine That Could" American Football League? Joe Namath did the smart thing before Super Bowl III. He believed in himself, which always seemed to work in his career.

Someone asked him his opinion of Earl Morrall, the Colts' quarterback, and he said Morrall would be a third-string quarterback on the Jets. He said the Jets were better than Baltimore, and he guaranteed that they would win. He sat out on a lounge chair at his Miami Beach hotel after practice, and he entertained the writers endlessly with his wit and counterculture wisdom.

Then he went out and beat the Colts. Beat them 16–7; it was 16–0 before Johnny Unitas engineered a late Baltimore score that ruined the shutout. Namath ran off the field, with his finger pointed skyward: We're No. 1. He walked away with the Most Valuable Player award, too.

And what a megastar he was. "He's the biggest thing in New York since Babe Ruth," Boston Patriot owner Billy Sullivan said in 1965. Namath lived in an Upper East Side penthouse apartment in Manhattan with a llama-skin rug and an oval bed and a marble bar—"I had the same decorator that Sinatra had for his pad," he once said proudly—and he tooled around New York in a gray Lincoln Continental. "Look man, I live and let live," he said when he was famous. "I like everybody. Why, I even like Howard Cosell." The man does tell it like it is.

REGGIE WHITE

On the day the Dallas Cowboys named Erik Williams their starting right tackle in 1992, he felt edgy. Not happy. Edgy. Because six weeks ahead of him was the job of blocking Philadelphia defensive end Reggie White. "My first thought was, I gotta get ready for Reggie," Williams says. "We weren't playing them till October, but even early in the season, I'd be watching extra film of him ... I mean, this was big, man."

Reggie White weighs 295 pounds. He stands 6' 5". He has the quickness of a safety and the brute strength of a powerlifter. When he leaves the game he will be remembered as one of the greatest defensive ends ever, and as the first very big free agent in the NFL's brave new world, which began in 1993. Entering the 1993 season he held the interesting and meaningful record of being the only player since the league has been keeping sack totals to have more sacks (124) than games played (121). "I don't think there's ever been a guy with the combination of size and speed and strength, ever, that Reggie White's had at that position," said veteran Cincinnati line coach Jim McNally.

Most of the great defensive linemen or linebackers in history have had one implicit job. They're supposed to disrupt quarterbacks' lives. The quarterback being the nerve center of a team, and the great defensive lineman or linebacker being charged with the task of stopping that team, the defensive player must make the quarterback's life miserable. White, for eight years in Philadelphia, did it almost every week. He was big enough to take on the 300-pound tackles in man-to-man combat and quick and fast enough to run around them to get to the passer.

Buddy Ryan, who coached the defense of the Bears, and the Jets and the Vikings before becoming Philly's head coach in 1985, saw White's abili-

ty quite early. "I've been around a lot of great defensive linemen, and Reggie's the best I've been around," Ryan said. "He's got better mobility than any of them. He's not just going to be good. He's going to be great."

Evidently the rest of the league thought so too when free agency came. At the age of 31 in the spring of 1993, White was courted by most teams in the league in need of defensive help—most, that is, with heavily greased palms. White would not come cheap. The Browns picked up White and his wife and agent in a private plane in Tennessee and ushered them to an $800-a-night suite atop the Ritz-Carlton Hotel in downtown Cleveland. They brought coaches and front-office people and some of the players to the Ritz for a recruiting dinner that night. The next day the Browns gave White's agent, Jimmy Sexton, the use of a private office at their practice complex so he could continue negotiating for his other players while White got to know the Browns. Cleveland owner Art Modell listened to White as he told of his desires to help inner-city kids through his personal ministry, and Modell thought he knew exactly how to get to White in a contract proposal: He would include a big chunk of change for the Reggie White ministry. The Browns' offer was for $12 million over four seasons, plus $2 million, spread out over 10 years, paid directly to White's charity work.

Great offer. Not great enough. The Packers offered White $17 million over four years, no strings attached. White decided that he could do ministry work just fine in Wisconsin for that kind of money.

"It's amazing how much the game's changed since I've started playing football," White said in the midst of wanton offers swirling around him. Reggie, you changed some of it yourself.

GEORGE BLANDA

With apologies to New England guard John Hannah, Green Bay running back Paul Hornung, Green Bay all-purpose player Johnny Blood from the '20s, Cleveland tackle Mike McCormack, San Francisco safety Ronnie Lott, Baltimore wide receiver Raymond Berry, New York Giant cornerback Emlen Tunnell and Giant linebacker Sam Huff, the 35th-best player of all time on our list is George Blanda, whose playing career of 26 years is the longest in NFL history.

You think Nolan Ryan has had some great times after reaching 40? He has. Gordie Howe did too, playing pro hockey with his kids. But the best year any athlete ever had in his '40s was had by George Blanda in 1970. A backup quarterback and kicker who had had an endless but fairly nondescript career to that point, Blanda, at age 43, began his impactful year in week six when quarterback Daryle Lamonica got hurt, with the Raiders a disappointing 2-2-1 and tied in this particular game with Pittsburgh 7–7. Blanda threw for three touchdowns, one on his very first play, and the Raiders won 31–14. The next week he lofted a 48-yard field goal through the uprights with three seconds left to salvage a 17–17 tie with defending AFL champ Kansas City. When he got back to Oakland, members of an Over-40 Fan Club wired him this telegram: "ON BEHALF OF ALL THE OTHER SENILE OLD WRECKS, WE SALUTE YOU!" Lamonica got hurt again the next week, against Cleveland, and Blanda had to rally the Raiders from a 20–13 deficit with four minutes left. He found Warren Wells for a touchdown after a 69-yard drive; after an Oakland interception, Blanda got the Raiders to the Cleveland 45 with three seconds left. He lined up for a 52-yard field goal, the longest he had ever tried in his career. And he hit it. On the

Oakland radio broadcast the announcer screamed, "George Blanda has just been elected king of the world!" That week the newspaper *The Catholic Voice* wrote that church attendance was rising because "so many Oakland fans were saying if he makes this one, I'm going back to church."

The next week the Raiders were stumbling offensively in Denver, trailing 19–17 with four minutes left, when John Madden sent Blanda in. He converted a third-and-12 from the Oakland 18 right away and then drove the Raiders 82 yards, tossing a scoring strike to Freddie Biletnikoff for the winning points. The next week the score was tied with San Diego with seven seconds left. It was fourth down. The Raiders had the ball on the Charger 16. "Could anyone in the whole world set the stage any more dramatically?" Raider broadcaster Bill King asked. No. The 23-yard field goal was perfect.

Five straight weeks. He won or tied games at the bitter end for five straight weeks. The producers of the TV show *Mission: Impossible* sent a telegram saying that Blanda was plagiarizing the show. Blanda quarterbacked the Raiders into the AFC Championship Game, but he had no more miracles in his helmet. He finished his career at the age of 48, with 2,002 points, the most by any player ever, and he told anyone who would listen—in 1970 and to this day—that he had no secrets.

"My special diet consists of the same things I've been eating since I grew up: steak and potatoes and green vegetables," he wrote in a *Sports Illustrated* story in 1971. "I smoke and drink ... [smoking] a pack or two a day, although I don't inhale them. As for alcohol, I enjoy bourbon. One of pro football's main unreasoning prejudices is that you're no longer capable of playing when you reach 30 or 35. Baloney!"

T E A M S

CLEVELAND BROWNS

1946 - 1955

Controversial choice. The best defense of it: The Browns played in their league championship game for 10 straight years ... and won seven times.

We don't want to hear about how the greatest team of all time is tainted. We don't want to hear, "They played four seasons in a bush league. What about the Lombardi Packers? What about Halas's Bears of the '30s and '40s?"

Fact is, the Browns would be among the top 10 teams of all time even if they hadn't played in the All-America Football Conference. But what they accomplished in the AAFC, and in the NFL in 1950, surely must be considered.

The AAFC, a forerunner of the AFL, was alive for

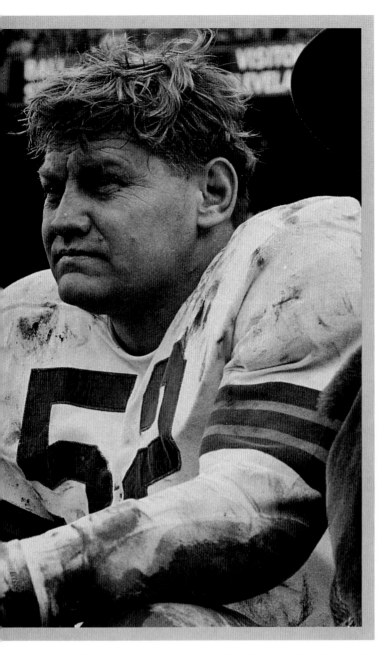

The Browns' powerful offensive line included Abe Gibron (64) and future Hall of Famer Frank Gatski (52).

In 1950 the Browns entered the NFL with a bounty on their collective helmet. When the NFL and AFL merged in 1970, the established NFL teams were gunning for the Jets and Chiefs, who had won the previous two Super Bowls. That first year the Jets finished 4–10 and the Chiefs 7-5-2. Well, with similar pressure in 1950, the Browns went 5–0 in the preseason. They played the defending NFL champions, Philadelphia, in the opening regular-season game of their first NFL year, at Philly, before 71,237 fans, and won 35–10. "Cleveland is the best football team I have ever seen," commissioner Bert Bell said that night. They followed a 10–2 regular season with an NFL title in the first year, and they won conference titles each of the next five seasons. They beat the Lions by 46 to win the 1954 title and the Rams by 24 to win in 1955.

Cleveland had the most innovative coach of his time (Brown), the best blocking-and-running back (Marion Motley) in football, the most precise and successful quarterback (Otto Graham), four future Hall of Fame offensive linemen (Frank Gatski, Mike McCormack, Bill Willis, Lou Groza), the best receiving corps of the day (Dub Jones, Mac Speedie, Dante Lavelli) and a Hall of Fame pass rusher (Len Ford).

They did have one Achilles heel, though. Entering the league championship game in 1954, they had lost to Detroit eight straight times—twice in the regular season, four times in the preseason and twice in the postseason. The Browns were getting old now. Motley, 34, was out with injuries. Graham, 33, had had a dreadful title game against Detroit the previous year. Lavelli, Ford, Willis and Gatski also had passed 30, and the Browns knew they were headed toward the twilight of their greatness. In the snow the previous week at Detroit, the Lions beat Cleveland 14–10 to close the regular season.

But in the title game Graham put the stamp of greatness on his career. He threw for three touchdowns. He ran for three. The Browns won 56–10. The next season, Graham's last, the Browns won their seventh championship in a decade, ripping the Rams 38–14.

Al Davis always says the mark of a truly great team is one that dominates its competition. These Browns won 84.2% of their regular-season games over a decade, and they won seven league championship games by an average of three touchdown a game. No team in history ever dominated the way the Browns did during the first decade after World War II.

four seasons, 1946 through '49. The quality of football, veteran observers said, was about what the quality of early American Football League ball would be a decade or so later. The Browns, under coach and general manager Paul Brown, traded for and acquired such a crew of talent that no one in the league could touch them. Cleveland won all four AAFC title games by an average of 18 points. The Browns went 34-1-3 in their last 38 AAFC games. Two days before their final AAFC game, in 1949, the Browns were accepted into the established league.

Greatest Teams

GREEN BAY PACKERS

1960 – 1967

What is most remarkable about this team is the man who built it. In 1958 the Packers finished with the worst record in their history, 1-10-1. In 1959 Vince Lombardi began molding and shaping and coaching what everyone thought was an awful club.

They might have been right. The quarterback, Bart Starr, was a pedestrian talent, and what was supposed to be a starry backfield, Paul Hornung and Jim Taylor, hadn't done anything in the NFL yet. All the defense had done was allow 32 points a game in 1958, the highest per-game average in Packer history. The stench in northeast Wisconsin was pretty powerful, and it wasn't from the paper mills.

Lombardi's greatest achievement with this group: Three years later, when the Packers won their first of five titles in seven years, 14 of the 22 starters were guys who'd been with the club in that awful 1958 season. Lombardi didn't come in and clear out the riffraff. He worked the riffraff. He challenged the riffraff. He physically and mentally beat up the riffraff. And suddenly, around 1960, they weren't riffraff anymore. They were contenders. And then they were champions.

The manner in which Lombardi gave this team football intelligence and will and an indomitable spirit is a lesson to any team in any sport. In the last 25 years, in all sports, Lombardi has become the authoritative source for coaches in search of an inspirational speech or a way to win against all odds or an example to prove that it's possible to take average talent and transform it into a championship unit. He said: "It takes a lot more of a man to perform as a champion than it did to get

The calm amid the storm: Lombardi (left) and Starr
enjoyed few such peaceful moments on the sidelines.

him there." He said: "Talent is not only a blessing. It is a burden, as the great ones find out." He said: "You will make mistakes, but not very many if you want to play for the Green Bay Packers." And he said lots of things with four-letter words included.

In many ways Lombardi has been misconstrued over the years as a taskmaster, plain and simple. "When he tells me to sit down, I don't even look for a chair," defensive tackle Henry Jordan said. But he taught the game so long and so hard to his players that it became a brutal kind of second nature. Each summer he began anew teaching the famed power sweep to his offense. The same stuff, year after year, kept getting drilled into old and new heads until it was as well known as shoe-tying.

In retrospect the Packer accomplishments under Lombardi are even more impressive than they seemed at the time. First, by whipping the Giants of the Frank Gifford era in the 1961 and 1962 championship games, they prevented the Giants from being one of the best teams ever. Second, they are the only team in the last 60 years to win three NFL championships in a row. Third, by winning the first two Super Bowls convincingly, they maintained NFL dominance when the upstart American Football League was challenging the old league.

When Starr won the fifth and final NFL title by muscling into a frozen end zone to beat Dallas in the 1967 championship game, Cowboy coach Tom Landry knew why he'd lost. "The discipline and conditioning programs they went through, the punishment and suffering, they all tend to develop character. And once you get character, you develop hope on all situations. Therefore, they never were out of a game. That is what beat us."

PITTSBURGH STEELERS

1972 - 1979

What a run of good fortune and great decision-making and phenomenal football this team had. Think of it. After the 1968 season the Rooneys decided that the Steelers needed a new coach. Joe Paterno of Penn State turned them down, so they had to settle for the Baltimore Colts' line coach, Chuck Noll. After the 1969 season they were in a coin toss with the Chicago Bears for the top pick of the 1970 draft. The Bears called heads. It came up tails. The Steelers got quarterback Terry Bradshaw. The hapless Bears traded their pick to Green Bay and got LeRoy Caffey, Elijah Pitts and Bob Hyland, who, combined, played a grand total of two seasons in Chicago.

The Steelers also had a nose for talent. They scouted black colleges extensively, and came away with L.C. Greenwood, Ernie Holmes and John Stallworth, none of them taken higher than the fourth round. They chose Franco Harris by a hair over Robert Newhouse in the 1972 draft. And in 1974 they had one of the greatest drafts ever, picking Lynn Swann, Jack Lambert, Stallworth and Mike Webster in the first five rounds.

And if ever luck and talent weren't enough, the Steelers had ingenuity to fall back on. Don't forget that. This was a crafty team. In 1974 offensive line coach Dan Radakovich was appalled at how light his linemen were; guards Gerry Mullins and Jim Clack weighed in at 222 and 218, respectively, late that season. Radakovich thought they were getting thrown around too much by big defensive linemen, so he had equipment manager Tony Parisi's mother-in-law tailor all the linemen's jerseys so tight that defensive players couldn't grab the cloth. And each Sunday he stuck the jerseys to the pads with double-sided tape.

It isn't like nothing ever went wrong. But the way the city loved this team, and the way everything they did turned to Steeler gold, it was like ... like....

"I still feel it to this day: It was like being in Camelot," said Art Rooney Jr., then the scouting director.

It started at the top, with a wonderful man, Art Rooney Sr., who lived the all-for-one, one-for-all life, fostering the harmony that characterized this team. There probably has never been a more beloved owner in sports history. During the 1974 strike he brought beer to picketing players, for crying out loud. In 1979, before a game at New England, Rooney was walking through the club hotel when he noticed that a standard hotel room was being prepared for a wedding. Rooney, who had his customary suite on this trip, stuck his head in the door. "This room's too small for a wedding," he said. "Use mine. I've got a suite." And he handed them the keys.

From 1972 through '79, the Steelers had a regular season record of 88-27-1. But their signature stretch happened in 1976, when they were gunning for their third straight Super Bowl title. They started the season 1–4, with Bradshaw hurt, and then, over the last nine games, their defense turned stifling. It shut out five opponents and yielded a total of 28 points. The offense scored 234. "How could you not win?" said linebacker Andy Russell. "We had an all-star team."

They lost to the Raiders in the AFC title game that year; Harris and Rocky Bleier had gotten hurt the week before and couldn't play. But Pittsburgh still won four Super Bowls in six years. The only team close to that record is San Francisco. But it took the Niners nine years to win four.

"What we had," Bradshaw said, "was an undeniable hatred of losing. We despised losing! Woe be to the fool who came into our stadium on Sunday. We had the fangs and the blood and the slobber! We loved it, Jack!"

Another year, another Super Bowl: Swann and Harris (32) celebrate the Steelers' third title, in Super Bowl XIII.

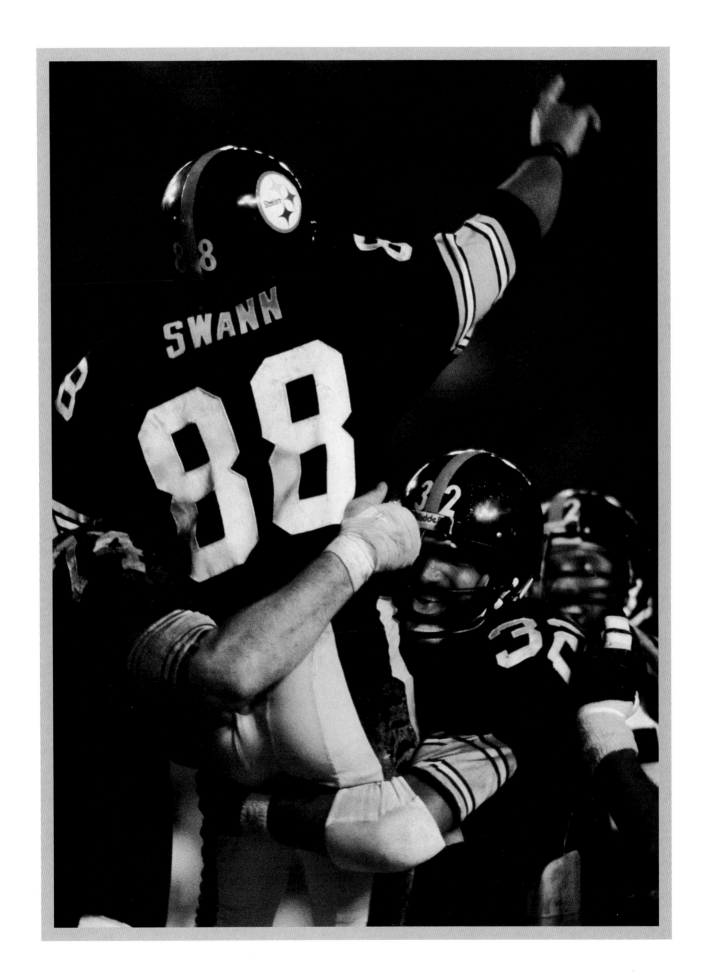

SAN FRANCISCO 49ERS

1981 - 1992

And they're still good.

That's the beauty of these 49ers. They changed on the fly, and they still contend for championships. Lose Joe Montana to Dwight Clark, gain Steve Young to Jerry Rice, with years of greatness remaining for both. Roger Craig and Wendell Tyler graduate; Ricky Watters and Tom Rathman enroll. So long, Sam Wyche, Paul Hackett, Mike Holmgren. Hello, Mike Shanahan. 'Bye, Bill Walsh. Hi, George Seifert.

If they win another Super Bowl or two this decade, you would almost have to move them up with the Browns. It would mean they had won big in both the Walsh-Montana era and the Seifert-Young era, bridged by the greatest day of drafting and trading in NFL history. The day: April 29, 1986. The trades: seven of them. One sent quarterback Matt Cavanaugh, a career backup, to Philadelphia for a second-round pick in 1987; that pick would be used as the primary bait for acquiring Young on draft day in 1987. The other six deals brought the 49ers a bunch of picks in rounds two through five of this draft, plus Washington's first-round choice in 1987. With all of their picks in 1986, they got future defensive-end starters Kevin Fagan and Larry Roberts, fullback Tom Rathman, wide receiver John Taylor, linebacker Charles Haley, tackle Steve Wallace and starting corners Tim McKyer and Don Griffin. Three time zones away, then-coach Bill Parcells of the Giants saw what was coming. "The 49ers might have just had one of the greatest drafts ever," Parcells said.

Before that day and after, they've been one of the most remarkable teams ever. And a clutch team. There was no legend of Joe Montana in January 1982, when the Cowboys, trying to hang on to the remnants of their greatness, went to Candlestick Park for the NFC Championship Game. Montana drove his team 90 yards in the last five minutes, the 49ers winning on a fingertip touchdown catch by Dwight Clark, who must have had epoxy glue on those fingers. In the Super Bowl a courageous goal line stand propelled them over Cincinnati. In 1984 the Niners were so great (15–1) that they just crushed people in the playoffs. Then they retooled and retooled some more—getting Rice and Young and Haley—and were good enough again in 1989 for Montana to win on a 92-yard drive in the final four minutes of Super Bowl XXIII. That one beat the Bengals again. They drilled Denver 55–10 in the first Super Bowl of the '90s, becoming the first team since the Steelers in '80 to win two titles in a row. They might have gone farther and done more but for

an inexcusable fumble and the Dallas Cowboys. Running out the clock with a 13–12 lead in the 1990 NFC title game against the Giants, Craig inexplicably fumbled, and the Giants won on a last-play field goal. And after cruising through the 1992 season 14–2 without Montana, the 49ers were beaten by young and starry Dallas in the NFC title game.

There was always immense talent on the 49er team, and something else too. There was a belief that, with Montana in back of center, anything was possible. We take you to the start of the fourth quarter of the 49ers' game at Philadelphia on Sept. 24, 1989. The Eagles led 21–10, and midway through the quarter, after Montana and Randall Cunningham each threw for touchdowns, San Francisco was still down 11, 28–17.

With six minutes left Montana threw an eight-yard touchdown pass to Tom Rathman. With just over three minutes left he hit Brent Jones with a 25-yard touchdown pass. With 2:02 left he iced it, hitting Rice for a 33-yard TD. Four minutes, three touchdown passes. The 49ers won 38–28.

In the end zone owner Eddie DeBartolo had tears streaming down his face. "I've never been prouder of these guys than I am right now, not even in the Super Bowl," he said, his voice cracking. Later, in the locker room, he hugged Montana. "I love you, Joe," he said.

So did a generation of fans.

Greatest 5 Teams

CHICAGO BEARS

1932 - 1943

What games, what stories, what names. Here's our Lettermanesque list of the top 10 stories about the best team from the years between the Depression and World War II:

10. The first three games of this era ended in 0–0 ties.

9. The first season ended inside Chicago Stadium because snow-covered Wrigley Field couldn't be cleared; the Bears beat Portsmouth 9–0 in the first, and, until the domes of the modern era, only indoor title game in NFL history, scoring on a Bronko Nagurski to Red Grange pass. The Bears' win does get one small asterisk: Dutch Clark, the Portsmouth quarterback and

the league's leading scorer, couldn't get time off from his job as a basketball coach in Colorado to play.

8. The second season ended with another Bear championship on the strangest title-game-deciding play ever. Nagurski threw a halfback option pass to end Bill Hewitt, who, about to be tackled, lateraled the ball to halfback Bill Karr, who scored to complete the 33-yard play. Bears 23, Giants 21.

7. Grange made the last tackle of the 1933 title game.

The Bears' bench erupted in celebration after the first of Chicago's 11 touchdowns in the 1940 title game.

6. In 1934 the Bears tried to win their third straight championship game on the icy tundra of the Polo Grounds. They slipped and slid to a 10–3 lead at half-time. The Giants sent out for sneakers at halftime because none of their players could get traction on the frozen field. In the second half the surefooted Giants ran past the Bears and won 30–13. That was the season's only blemish for the Bears, who had been 13–0.

5. In the 1937 Chicago-Washington championship game at Wrigley Field, Redskin owner George Preston Marshall became enraged when he saw a Bear take a swing at his great rookie quarterback, Sammy Baugh. Marshall ran from his 50-yard-line box seat to challenge Chicago coach George Halas on the sideline. "Get up in that box where you belong!" Halas sneered. "It's too bad it ain't a cage!" Washington won 28–21.

4. In 1937 Nagurski doubled as a professional wrestler ... during the season. He wrestled as far east as Philadelphia, west as Los Angeles, south as Phoenix and north as Vancouver.

3. In 1940 the Bears lost a late-season game at Washington 7–3, then went back to Washington three Sundays later to play the NFL title game. Chicago edged Washington 73–0. "Some observers said the Bears were a perfect team that day," Halas said years later. "I can't quite agree. Looking over the movies, I can see where we should have scored another touchdown."

2. In 1941 a season ticket on the 50-yard-line for the Bears' six home games cost $10.80. The defending champs also got a fight song that year, "Bear Down, Chicago Bears," written by the immortal Al Hoffman. He's the guy who wrote: "If I Knew You Were Coming, I'd Have Baked a Cake." Two weeks after the United States entered World War II, the Bears beat the Giants 37–9 to win their fourth title of this era.

1. With the Bears cruising to a 6–0 record in early November 1942, Naval Reserve officer George Halas left the team for active war duty. Young Bussey, the Bears' backup quarterback, went too. Halas came back. Bussey didn't; he was killed in battle in the Philippines in January 1945. Without Halas the Bears lost the 1942 title game to Washington but came back the next year to beat the Redskins in the title game.

At the beginning of this era the NFL was still struggling for credibility. At the end of the era the NFL had it. For the Bears' preseason game against the college all-stars in 1942, a crowd of 101,100 came to Soldier Field.

MIAMI
DOLPHINS

1 9 7 0 – 1 9 7 4

Don Shula can be a domineering guy, but that happens mostly around his team, and only because he takes the game so seriously. In social settings the longtime coach of the Miami Dolphins can be downright endearing. And so it was with little trepidation that the president of NFL Films, Steve Sabol, picked up the phone in his New Jersey office and found Shula on the other end. Always nice to hear from his good pal Don, Sabol thought.

"How in the world could you not pick us the best team of all time?" Shula said.

This was several years ago, and NFL Films had just played a fake tournament to determine the best team of all time. Sabol had arranged for some computer whiz to throw the data from all the great teams in NFL history into the computer, the result being that two teams from the '70s, the '78 Steelers and the '72 Dolphins, "won" their way into the championship game. Shula sat down and watched this hypothetical game on TV, with trick footage spliced together to create the appearance that the two teams were really playing each other. Now, in reality, late in 1972, when much of the great Steeler team was already in place, the Dolphins had won the AFC Championship Game at Pittsburgh 21–17. So Shula was fairly sure as he plopped down to watch this invented game, that the Dolphins would be crowned the greatest ever. Nope. The Steelers won. Shula growled. Sabol learned.

"Last time I'll ever do this," Sabol said with genuine regret in his voice. To this day his old pal Shula still looks at him a little funny.

For one season the Dolphins were arguably the best team ever. In 1972, a year after losing Super Bowl VI to the Dallas Cowboys, the Dolphins became the only team on NFL record—no one has matched them

The No-Name Defense included Bob Heinz (72), Nick Buoniconti (85) and Manny Fernandez (75).

since—to have an unbeaten, untied season. Roll that around for a while. It seems amazing that it hasn't happened more than once in the 74-year history of the NFL, but Miami, at 17-0-0 in 1972, is the only unblemished team of all time. It may be that the Dolphins don't get the respect they deserve because they didn't roll through the '72 playoffs: they beat Cleveland by six, Pittsburgh by four and Washington by seven. Or because they didn't sustain their greatness;

they went 15–2 and won another Super Bowl the year after the perfect season, and then they went eight years without winning another playoff game ... in part because of developments beyond Shula's control. The World Football League sprang up in 1974 and stole three of Miami's premier weapons: fullback Larry Csonka, halfback Jim Kiick and wide receiver Paul Warfield.

This was a classic team of role players. Bob Griese was certainly not the best quarterback of his day, but he was maddeningly accurate and had zero ego. The ground game churned perfectly behind the strongest and most technically perfect line of its era, with Csonka and Kiick grinding out the tough yards and Mercury Morris bursting to a 1,000-yard season in 1972. Warfield stretched defenses, although he caught but 29 balls in the perfect season. The defense, whose very moniker—the No-Name Defense—bespoke a lack of star power, had a different standout every week. The star of Super Bowl VII, for instance, was the team's 11th-leading tackler, safety Jake Scott, who intercepted two Redskin passes. How fitting: Scott is now an almost forgotten figure, yet he was the MVP of the game that capped the only perfect season ever.

Greatest *7* Teams

CANTON
BULLDOGS

1922 – 1923

Judging the worthiness of the Canton Bulldogs to be included among the greatest pro football teams is like judging Abner Doubleday's importance in baseball history. You know Doubleday had something to do with inventing baseball, but you're not exactly sure what it is. History is that fuzzy. You know, by looking at Canton's record, that the Bulldogs belong on the list. But where precisely?

Your decision is complicated by the way business was conducted in the early years of the National Football League. Since there was no draft or organized distribution of players, players were bought and sold from club to club in the chummy Midwestern NFL, which stretched from Buffalo to Green Bay. In 1923 Jim Thorpe began the year as player-coach of the Oorang Indians (who, by the way, were all Native Americans

In 1920 the Bulldogs (with the C on their jerseys) took on the Buffalo All Americans in the Polo Grounds.

and ran onto the field each week in full headdress) in Marion, Ohio. The Indians folded when the Oorang dog kennel, the club's sponsor, withdrew its financial support after their record fell to 1–10, and Thorpe just signed on with the nearby Toledo Maroons. Player-coach George Halas of the Chicago Bears came to admire a great tackle for the Rock Island (Ill.) Independents named Ed Healey after playing against him. Halas offered Rock Island $100 for Healey, and the Independents accepted the deal. Today that would be like player-coach Jim Lachey of the Washington Redskins admiring the skills of Green Bay lineman Reggie White so much that a few days after the game Lachey

buys White from Green Bay. Weird. And the respect the league had was almost nil. "In the '20s," says current New York Giants president Wellington Mara, a grade-schooler then, "pro football players were held in the regard that professional wrestlers are held today. No one thought much of the game or the players."

The best story in the early years of the league, though, happened in Green Bay. The league president, a sportsman from Columbus, Ohio, named Joe Carr, disciplined the Packers harshly for playing active college players in 1921 under assumed names. Carr revoked Green Bay's franchise, refunding the $50 franchise fee to the Acme Packing Co., of Green Bay. In 1922 a player-coach named Curly Lambeau reapplied for the Green Bay franchise, promising to do nothing outside the rules, and the league agreed to give Lambeau the team. Lambeau had the franchise fee but not the money for his fare to Canton, where he needed to file his application. So a friend, Don Murphy, sold his car to pay the fare and in exchange was allowed to start the Packers' first game of 1922, at tackle. After one minute of play, Murphy retired for good.

The point is, we'll never know how good these Bulldogs were, because of the sketchiness of league records—many scores of games in those days simply can't be found—and the inconsistency of opponents. We do know a few things. Wiry coach and end Guy Chamberlin, a teammate of George Halas's with the Chicago Staleys in 1921, moved to the small northeast Ohio city of Canton to run the team. A couple of two-way tackles, Fats Henry and Link Lyman, controlled both lines of scrimmage. Henry might have been the league's MVP in 1922 if such an award had existed. He punted and kicked too, and his 50-yard dropkick field goal against title contender Toledo in November 1922 will probably never be matched.

The Bulldogs, 10-0-2 in 1922, beat out the two Chicago teams, the Bears (9–3) and the Cardinals (8–3), for the title. In 1923 Henry and Lyman stopped the Bears cold, 6–0, in the match that helped decide the league champion. The 1923 Bulldogs were 11-0-1. In 1924 the Bulldogs, in search of bigger crowds, moved north to Cleveland and won another title. A tainted title it was: Cleveland and runner-up Frankford (Pa.) both scheduled late-season games against nonleague cupcakes to boost their records; Carr ruled the games invalid and declared Cleveland the champion. Strange, but true ... just like the early years of the NFL.

Greatest **8** Teams

OAKLAND/
L.A. RAIDERS

1967 – 1985

If an Oscar were to be named in honor of the Raiders, it would have to be awarded for lifetime achievement. The Raiders are the Liz Taylor, the Jimmy Stewart, of professional football. From 1967 to 1977 they won at least twice as many as they lost, every year. Maybe, just maybe, they kept the Steelers from being the best team of all time; they kayoed Pittsburgh in the 1973 and '76 playoffs, bookending the Steelers' first two Super Bowl seasons. Then, in 1981, when they were supposed to have started on their downhill slide with a 7–9 season, they revved it up one more time. They had the best record in the AFC in 1982, won the Super Bowl in 1983, had an 11–5 Wild Card season in 1984 and won another division title in 1985. During the first 20 years of Super Bowl competition, the Raiders made it to the AFC or AFL title game an astonishing 11 times, more than any other team in football. Four of those times resulted in appearances in the big game.

As long as we're in Hollywood, let's figure out who Raider owner Al Davis is. Make it Bond.... James Bond. That's the guy. His reputation today, rightfully, has been dulled by almost a decade of mediocrity. But the league still looks over its shoulder at him. The league office thinks Al is arrogant. Al thinks the league office is arrogant. General managers still think thrice about trading with the guy. There's a paranoia about dealing with Davis that just won't go away. He does anything to get an edge. Even in 1993, when real free agency hit pro football, Davis tried in his own picayune way to get an edge. He sent a Raider operative to Minneapolis to study the Minnesota Twins organization. Never mind that the Twins don't play football. "The Twins," Davis reasoned, "have probably handled the transient nature of sports better

Four key Raiders: fullback Marv Hubbard, wide receiver Fred Biletnikoff, kicker-QB George Blanda and Stabler.

than any other team. They always seem to be able to contend."

What makes the Raiders so special is that they won in different eras, with different teams, with different coaches, with different casts. In the generation from from 1963 to '84, the best winning percentage in sports was the Raiders' .715; the next-best winning percentage, the Dallas Cowboys', was .693; the next best in other sports, the Montreal Canadiens', was .666. The American baby boomer generation grew up

watching the Raiders win on more than seven of 10 Sundays, year in and year out.

They won with strangely contrasting quarterbacks and coaches. This era started with quarterback Daryle Lamonica, who was so organized that he wrote out his game plan by hand the night before games. Then they won with fiery Ken Stabler calling signals; the night before games all he wrote was women's phone numbers on cocktail napkins. Then they won with Jim Plunkett and even for a while with Marc Wilson calling plays, though neither was a forceful personality. They went 16–1 in 1976 and won a Super Bowl with boisterous John Madden coaching. They went 15–4 in 1983 and won a title under the bookish leadership of Tom Flores. They won in Oakland, and in the first two tumultuous years after moving to L.A., they went 24–6.

They won with a vertical pass offense, the one that looked outmoded and seemed to drag them down in the '90s, and they won with one of the meanest defenses the league has ever seen. Mean might be a nice word for it. "The Raider defense is based on the three P's—pointing, pushing and punching," linebacker Matt Millen said in 1983.

They won, period. Which is all Al Davis ever wanted to do, his whole life. "Just win, baby," was his slogan. For a generation, that's practically all they did.

GREEN BAY PACKERS

1929 – 1932

No town has ever fought as hard to keep a team as Green Bay did in the early years of the NFL, and no team deserved the championships quite as much. When the Packers had to come up with money to get re-started in 1922, a friend of player-coach Curly Lambeau sold his car so he could contribute $50 to the cause. In the '30s a man fell from the stands at a Packer game, sued the organization, won $5,000 and put the Packers into bankruptcy; Green Bay businessmen raised $15,000 to pay off debtors and reorganize the team.

There was a loyalty, then, from team to town and town to team. The players loved the place, and the

place loved them back. While other teams juggled their rosters every year, the Pack was a constant: Of the 23 players on the 1929 title team, 14 were still regulars on the 1931 championship team.

The league didn't make it easy on them. The NFL tried to schedule the Packers at home for most of September and October, and on the road for most of November and December, theorizing that the weather would be intolerable up north late in the season. And

The '31 squad included Hall of Famers Lambeau (back row, far left) and quarterback Arnie Herber (back row, far right).

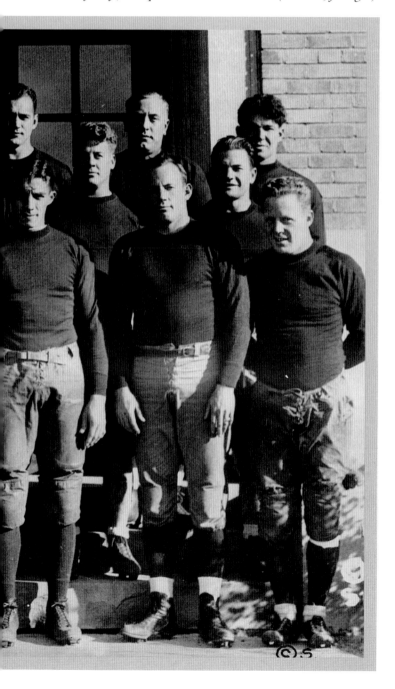

there was no guarantee a team would play as many games at home as it did on the road. In 1929 the Packers played 13 games—the first five at home, the last eight on the road. Same thing in 1930: Six of their first seven games were played at home, then seven straight away. In their three straight championship seasons the Packers played at home only twice after October. And so they had to start fast, yet still have enough strength left when the long grind of the road got to them. They did, starting 10–0 in 1929, 8–0 in '30 and 9–0 in '31.

In fact, the more you read about the conditions of the day, the more impressed you are that a team could string so many wins together. On Nov. 23, 1930, the Packers lost a Sunday game to the Giants at the Polo Grounds 13–6. Four days later, in suburban Philadelphia, they drilled the Frankford Yellow Jackets 25–7. Three days later the Packers, desperately needing a win to ensure an advantage for the NFL title, played the Staten Island Stapletons. In uniform they bused from their Manhattan hotel to the Staten Island Ferry, took the trip to the island and walked about a mile from the ferry to the football grounds. Green Bay's talent won out over fatigue in a 37–7 win over the Stapes.

In 1929 the Green Bay faithful were rewarded with what might be the best defensive season any professional team has ever had. In 13 games the Packers allowed a total of 22 points. They shut out their first two foes and their last three. They did it, in large part, because their wunderkind player/coach/general manager, Lambeau, acquired great players to fortify a team made up mostly of northeastern Wisconsin fellows. The barnstorming New York Yankees, led by gate attraction Red Grange, folded after the 1928 season, and Lambeau grabbed stalwarts Cal Hubbard, a two-way tackle, and Mike Michalske, another lineman, from the remains. Johnny Blood, a halfback and defensive back, came when the Pottsville (Pa.) franchise folded. Hubbard, Michalske and Blood all became Packer stars and all went to the Pro Football Hall of Fame.

The killer schedule and the rest of the league eventually caught up with the visionary Lambeau. But even so the Packers should have won a fourth straight title. In 1932 the Bears were declared league champions with a 7-1-6 record, ahead of the 10-3-1 Packers because in those days league standings were decided on winning percentages; ties didn't count. (Theoretically, a 1-0-13 team would have won out over a 13–1 team.) Today, rightly, ties count as half a win and half a loss.

DETROIT LIONS

1952 – 1957

You had to like Buddy Parker of Kemp, Texas. Buddy Parker made football simple. Of course, his peers in the early '50s in the NFL used to say, I'd like to have Buddy Parker's simple plays with his great talent, with the best guard in football, Dick Stanfel, blocking for great weapons like halfback Doak Walker and quarterback Bobby Layne. But Parker, the coach of the Detroit Lions from 1951 through '56, coached by letting the talent of the players come out. Buddyisms we have loved:

•On coaching: "If you ask me, what ruins most teams is overcoaching. I can sit here in my office and think up plays by the yard. You set up an offense and you think, 'I better add this play,' and some assistant coach says, 'Let's put this in.' What about the players out there on the line of scrimmage who have to solve these masterpieces on the spur of the moment? Why bumfoozle them? You don't outmaneuver teams in this league. You beat them with good solid blocking and tackling."

•On practice: "We do 90 minutes early in the season and later in the year cut it to an hour. I found out long ago that you don't beat the enemy on Sunday by murdering each other on Wednesday."

•On his ability as a coach: "What's the use of kidding ourselves? You've got to have the players ... and new blood every year."

Detroit's Leon Hart, the former Notre Dame star end, put it perfectly about Parker, comparing him to the Fighting Irish coach Frank Leahy: "Leahy was a master at handling boys. Parker has that same faculty for handling men."

Detroit was a caldron of dissension when Parker took over in 1951. But he simplified the offense and defense, treated the players like adults and coached them easily. The Lions beat Cleveland for back-to-back titles behind Layne in 1952 and '53, plummeted to the bottom of the league for one season in 1955, and roundhoused the Browns with their last great team in 1957 for their third NFL championship. Interestingly, Parker had quit the club during training camp, saying, "The material is all right, but the team is dead." Suitably awakened, the Lions marched through the regular season 8–4, won a division playoff with San Francisco, and then faced the Browns, their archest of rivals, in their fourth championship meeting of the decade. Tobin Rote, acquired early in the season to platoon with Layne (who was on his way down, and didn't help matters with a drunk-driving arrest early in the season), quarterbacked the Lions to the championship game. And the fact was, Cleveland wasn't the same Cleveland without Otto Graham throwing and Marion Motley hammering the defense. Even when Cleveland was the best team in football earlier in the decade, the Lions were the only team to beat the Browns consistently.

Well, in the 1957 title game they beat the Browns consistently, all right. They beat them up, pummeling and humiliating the once proud Browns. The Lions were up 31–7 at the half. They won the second half 28–7. With seven different Lions scoring touchdowns, including two by rookie end Steve Junker, Detroit won the game 59–14. "This is the fightingest team I ever saw," said coach George Wilson. On his way out of the locker room that day, a fan bellowed to Wilson, "Hey coach! You murdered 'em!" The Lions got used to that in the '50s.

The 1951 Lions' backfield included (left to right): Layne, Ollie Cline, Bob Hoernschemeyer and Walker.

ARCHITECTS

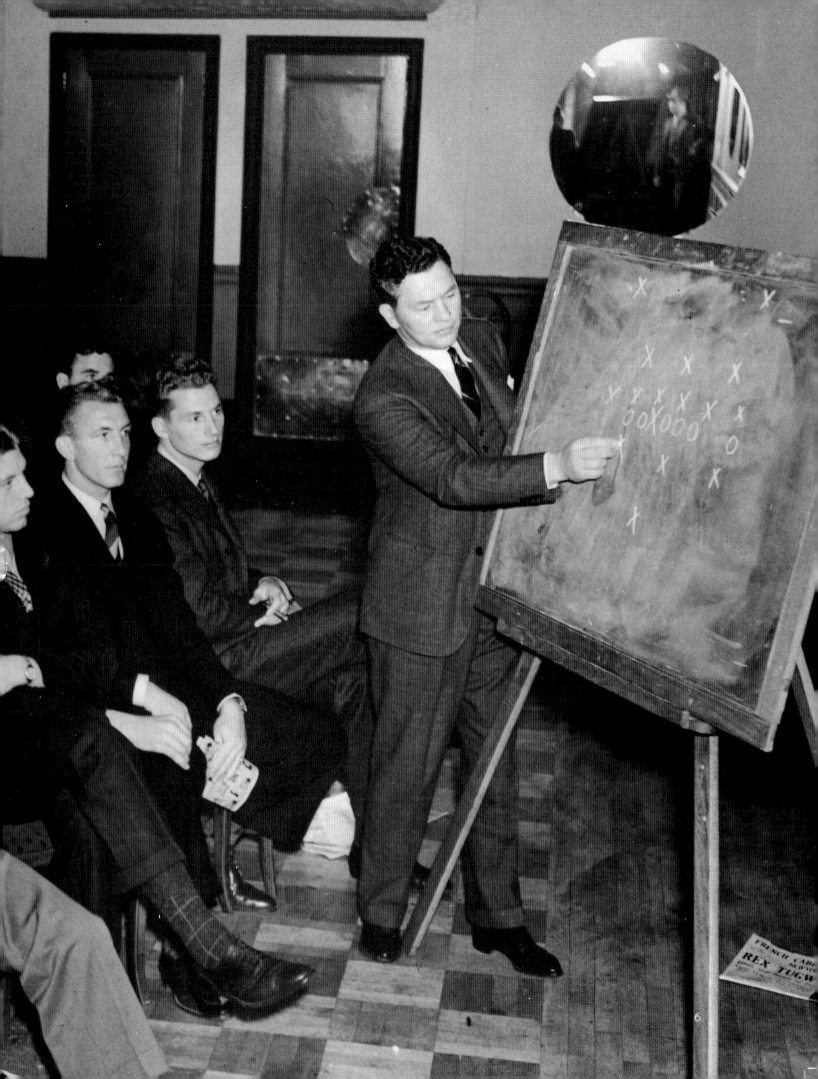

GEORGE HALAS

Even in his declining years George Halas was filled with a verve for life and for football that is unmatched in the game's history. At the age of 82, back in 1977, Halas was still working 10-hour days at the Chicago Bears' offices—five hours on Saturdays—even though the team was basically on automatic pilot by then, run by his protégés. At lunch he would read the *Wall Street Journal* and other financial publications, figuring out where to invest the team's money, and his own. He would stay up late Monday nights, scouting the NFL game on TV, charting the plays himself.

"I have no need to search for hobbies or outside interests," Halas said in 1977. "I have them all."

No distractions? No pleasures outside football? No vices?

"Look," he said. "You can have a session with your girlfriend. What's that last you? Twenty minutes? Half an hour? Or you can go out and get stiff with the boys. A few hours, right? But to win a game in the National Football League! That lasts a whole week! What a thrill! What a thrill!"

Let us talk for a moment about all the things George Halas did to make pro football the game it is today.

He founded the franchise in 1920. He sat in a new-car showroom in Canton, Ohio, and forked over $100 as the franchise fee for a pro football team in Chicago.

He coached Sid Luckman and Gale Sayers, Bronko Nagurski and Dick Butkus. He signed Red Grange. He drafted Walter Payton.

He returned a Jim Thorpe fumble an NFL-record 98 yards for a touchdown in a win over the Oorang Indians in 1923, outracing Thorpe to the end zone.

He was the first coach in professional football to hold practice sessions daily.

He spurred the league to split into two divisions in 1933, with the winners meeting annually for a scheduled championship game; none had been played previously. And he pushed that same year for forward passes to be permitted from anywhere behind the line of scrimmage, instead of from at least five yards behind the line; the league agreed. As early as the '40s Halas was scouring small colleges for talent and got two all-league players, center Bulldog Turner from Hardin-Simmons and receiver Harlon Hill from Florence Teachers College in Alabama.

He coached the Bears for five different terms, the first commencing in 1920, the last concluding in '67. He finished his career with more wins than anyone in pro football history—325. Only six of the 40 teams he coached finished below .500. Under Halas the Bears won six NFL titles.

Halas was Joe Gibbs long before there was a Joe Gibbs, napping on his office couch and working the Bears' game plan until 11:30 p.m. on nights early in the week. Every Monday he would call his quarterback—Luckman, often—at 11 p.m., telling him the plays he would have to know for that week's practices and games. That was in the '40s! Today we think it's real dedication when a quarterback gets the plays faxed to him on Tuesday and has a chance to study them before the practice week starts on Wednesday.

In sum, then, here's what George Halas did: He founded a cornerstone NFL team when the league was born. He coached it, and he played for it. He coached championship teams at the age of 26 and at the age of 68. He made league rules and established coaching practices that future generations of coaches would follow. There isn't a single man alive or dead who did more than George Halas to make pro football the national obsession it is today.

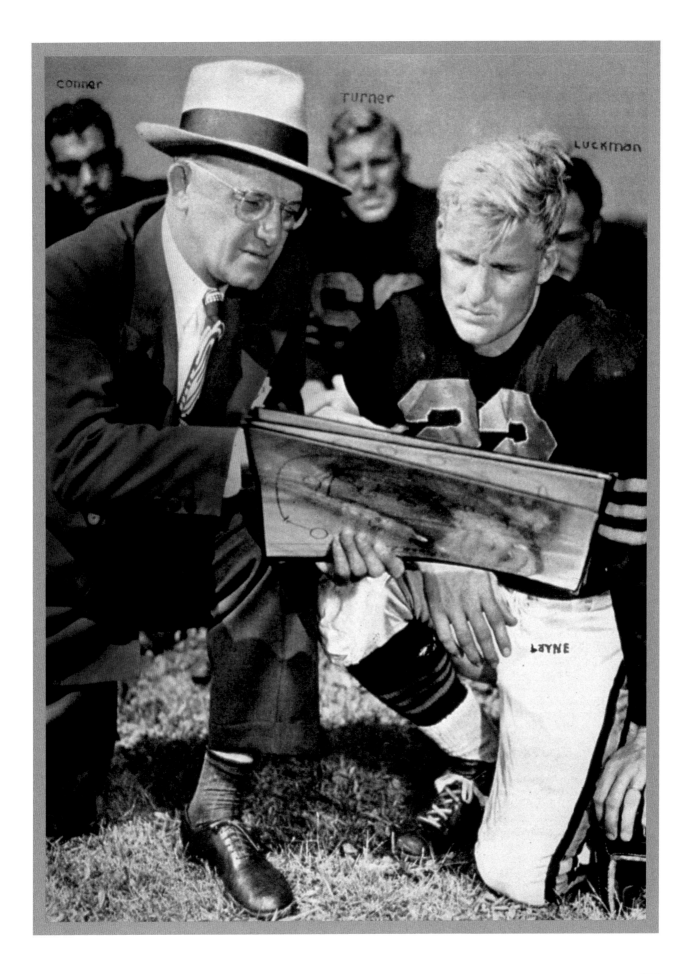

conner

Turner

Luckman

Layne

JOE CARR

Who?

Joe Carr never played the game. He was a small man with glasses from Columbus, Ohio, who believed pro football could be big. Monstrously big. Long before Kevin Costner heard a voice, Joe Carr was hearing one: If you build it, they will come. Beginning in 1920, Carr built it—the organization, the structure, the respect—and they came. By the time he died, of a heart attack in 1939, the infrastructure for pro football was established, and the game was on track for greatness.

Carr was a semipro football team manager in Columbus in 1919 when he began pressing the barnstorming teams to unite, quit roaming from town to town, and form a major league, with proper schedules and contracts for players. He pushed for a meeting in Canton, Ohio, in September 1920 which most of the major football figures of the day—Curly Lambeau from Green Bay, George Halas from Chicago, Jim Thorpe from Canton—attended. They formed the American Professional Football Association and asked Carr to be president. He said no. "I'm an unknown," Carr said. He pushed Thorpe for the job, and the owners agreed. A year later Thorpe gave way to Carr, who changed the league's name to the National Football League in 1922 and drew up a standard players' contract to give the league stability.

"In the beginning pro football was pretty much a catch-as-catch-can operation," George Halas recalled years later. "A guy would be on your team one week and playing against you the next. Ask him why and he'd say, 'Because they offered me five dollars more.' Before Joe came along, teams and football leagues were run by coaches and ex-players. Joe had what the rest of us lacked, and that was a real business sense. Joe said our real concern should be the future of the sport."

By introducing player contracts Carr eliminated the transient nature of the sport. He created a schedule so that teams couldn't play cupcake after cupcake. And he gave the league some honor. At the league's annual meeting in 1922, he presented proof that the Green Bay Packers had violated league rules by using college players under assumed names. "I realize you've all been guilty," Carr told the assembled owners and coaches. "But the only team I've caught red-handed is Green Bay. I am hereby declaring the Green Bay franchise forfeited. Any future violations will be dealt with in the same way." Lambeau got the franchise back eventually, but the ruling solidified Carr's power and authority. In 1925 he expelled the Milwaukee Badgers from the league for using high school players. When colleges expressed their outrage over Red Grange's leaving school early to barnstorm with the Chicago Bears, Carr forbade pro teams to raid college teams until a collegian's class had graduated.

In the 1930s Carr oversaw the creation of an annual championship game and the beginning of a college draft. By the late '30s he had taken a league of small-town teams and presided over its transformation into a thriving big-city league, with every major northern city east of the Mississippi exposed to the pro game.

In 1934 club owners gave Carr a 10-year contract, which he never got to fulfill. In the last NFL game before his death, though, the sport proved it was well on its way to greatness. With 48,120 watching in the Polo Grounds and Packer legend Don Hutson keying the Green Bay air game, the Giants survived a late scare to win the 1938 NFL Championship Game, 23–17. Big crowds. Big names. Big-city champions. Carr kickstarted the NFL to where it is today.

Architects

PAUL BROWN

When Sam Wyche took the Cincinnati Bengals' coaching job late in 1983, there were snickers all around the league. This unproven college coach is the only guy Paul Brown can get to coach his team, the whispers said. Who would want to coach a team with Brown, the founder and general manager and film-dissector and ultimate quiet presence, hovering over your shoulder the whole time? And it was true. Not many coaches would have enjoyed coaching under Brown, because coaches tend to want to run their ships their way, with a minimum of interference. Wyche actually sought out Brown's advice and urged him to watch film with the coaching staff. "Coaching under Paul Brown," Wyche said once, "is like living next to a library. I'd be a fool not to check any books out."

Brown, a famous high school and college coach in Ohio in the 1930s and '40s, took his clipboard to the Cleveland Browns—named after him—of the All-American Football Conference in 1946. Folks in the AAFC rubbed their hands together with glee at the thought of playing Brown's Browns, because he loaded his team with a bunch of kids he had known from high school and college ball. What's more, he signed and played blacks, the first coach to do that in a big way. All the Browns did was win every one of the four AAFC championships that were held. Then, in their maiden game after being accepted into the NFL in 1950, the Browns beat the defending champion Philadelphia Eagles 35–10 and went on to win the NFL title that same year. In all Brown coached and managed the Browns to 10 straight championship game appearances in the AAFC and NFL from 1946 to '55, adding NFL titles in 1954 and '55.

Brown founded the Bengals in 1968. Run on a relative shoestring with a tiny office staff and no off-season strength and conditioning program (heresy!), the Bengals made the Super Bowl twice under Brown's management.

Brown invented the face mask and the draw play. He instituted playbooks, training camps, college scouting, full-time coaching staffs and the use of offensive linemen to messenger in plays. A calm, thoughtful man, Brown railed against the excesses of modern football. "Some of my best thinking always came in the morning after a good rest," he said in 1988, three years before his death.

He might have been the shrewdest trader in NFL history. In 1948 he got wide receiver Dub Jones in a trade from Brooklyn for a player he would have cut. Jones became a Pro Bowl receiver. In 1984 he traded fat and washed-up Pete Johnson to San Diego for the fresh legs of James Brooks, who became the Bengals' alltime rushing leader.

"Paul was the last of his breed, an innovator who bridged the gap from the '30s to the '90s," Bill Walsh, a protégé, wrote after Brown's death. "No one—not Halas or Lombardi or Rozelle—can make that claim in the history of pro football."

Walsh, a Cincinnati assistant for eight seasons under Brown, took Brown's lessons to the 49ers in 1979. San Francisco became a great road team, the best in football in the 1980s and early '90s. "Bill Walsh drilled into us that we were on a business trip, that it was us against the world, 45 of us against a whole city," former San Francisco center Randy Cross said once, when asked why the 49ers did so well on the road.

Funny. Walsh also wrote when Brown died: "On the road ... it was 50 of us versus the 50,000 of them. This is a business trip, nothing more and nothing less."

The librarian has spoken.

PETE ROZELLE

League powers couldn't find a commissioner in 1960 after the death of Bert Bell. They really couldn't. None of the owners wanted the position. Paul Brown said he didn't want it. And nobody wanted the no-name Milquetoast league treasurer, Austin Gunsel, to have the job. The league seemed rudderless, a league without a leader.

There was an industrious 33-year-old general manager in the league at the time, Pete Rozelle of the Rams. Rozelle had extensive experience in public relations and newspaper work, but his tenure as G.M. wasn't going famously. He had sent quarterback Norm Van Brocklin to Philadelphia in 1958, and Van Brocklin won a championship with the Eagles two years later. He acquired running back Ollie Matson for nine players in 1959, but when Matson got to the Rams it was clear he was closer to the end of his career than Rozelle had realized. By the end of 1959 the Rams had lost eight straight games. Surely Rozelle was the last guy anybody would put up for commissioner.

But that's what Wellington Mara, the president of the Giants, did. Mara liked the young man's honesty and energy and spunk and know-how, and he went to Pittsburgh owner Art Rooney after the owners' 23rd vote had failed to elect a commissioner by the required three-quarters majority. "What about Pete Rozelle?" Mara said. Rooney was dubious but promised to ask influential Philadelphia owner Frank McNamee.

McNamee said, "Who is Pete Rozelle?"

Well, here's who he is, from one of the people who, for better or worse, got to know him well during his 29-year tenure as commissioner. "Pete Rozelle," said former NFL Players Association boss Ed Garvey, "has made the National Football League the first enterprise in America, in all the world, to have achieved absolute pure socialism."

Rozelle did a better job of walking the fine line between what's right and what's profitable than any commissioner the league ever had. He made the NFL the most popular sports league ever.

Early on it was easy, with the help of some magnanimous owners. Rozelle gave each team an equal share of the TV pie, which the owners thought was fine. Green Bay thus makes $32 million a year from TV, the same as the New York teams do, even though the New Yorkers obviously deliver more fans to more TVs. Consequently the league suffered none of the problems of inequity that plague baseball. In 1962, when the 35-year-old commissioner told the intimidating Vince Lombardi that he was about to suspend his best back, Paul Hornung, because of gambling, Lombardi did not complain. The early years were filled with consensus.

That ended as the '60s did. Rozelle steered the league into a merger with the pesky American Football League, and it was then that he learned how difficult his stewardship could be. "No matter how much you stroke them," he once said of the owners, "it's never enough." The owners couldn't agree on which old-line NFL teams should join the new American Football Conference to balance the two newly formed conferences at 13 teams apiece. The meeting to decide realignment lasted days. The following year produced another controversy—this one over the new, divisional league structure. This time Rozelle, tired of the bitter debate, ordered that all the alignments that had some support be written on pieces of paper and put in an office vase. Then he ordered his secretary to pull one out. The result became reality.

Rozelle had his battles royale—with Al Davis, the players union, Donald Trump—but he always came out with his honor intact. He was a strong captain as the NFL's lucrative ship came in.

AL DAVIS

Al Davis will forever be remembered as something akin to a CIA operative. Winning was Davis's paranoid mantra, and nothing in his business life ran even a close second. Get in his way, and he would squash you like a squirrel in the road.

We will get to that side of Davis. But first let's get to the side that deserves to be remembered more warmly, from the mouth of a longtime rival.

"Al Davis is unique in the modern era," said Sam Rutigliano, the former coach of the Cleveland Browns. "Look at all the hats he's worn—scout, coach, assistant coach, G.M., owner, even commissioner. Don't forget he was once the AFL commissioner. How many guys have gone to the owners meetings one week and walked the sidelines at a college practice the next? Maybe George Halas was like that in the old days, but this is a different era."

Davis helped the AFL quickly become a peer of the NFL because he built such great teams in Oakland and because he competed so aggressively with his NFL counterparts for players. Eight Raiders, including Davis himself, have made the Pro Football Hall of Fame; only the Steelers of the '70s can match that, and many of the Raiders in the Hall had played several years without fanfare in the early AFL. He embodied defiance in the men's club known as the NFL, because he dared to move his club from Oakland to Los Angeles in 1982. There can be no argument about this: Al Davis is the most controversial figure in the history of pro football. But don't forget that he built the greatest team over the longest span of modern football history. The Raiders went 198-70-7 in the 19 seasons from 1967 to '85.

The paranoia factor helped. It's only a slight exaggeration to say that Davis trusted no one and no one trusted him, almost from the day he took over as Raider coach and general manager in 1963.

He wanted opponents to fear him and his team, an attitude he learned from his endless study of military history and, of all things, the great New York Yankees. He understood how much armies feared the German war machine of the '30s and how baseball teams quaked upon entering Yankee Stadium. "Attack, fear, pressure," Davis once said, summing up his philosophy on offense. "Don't take what they give you. You're going deep, and they're not going to stop you by design or location. They say they can stop us? Prove it."

Now for the fun stuff. In 1968 Davis snuck a construction crew into Shea Stadium the night before the AFL Championship Game with the Jets to put a heater near the Oakland bench. Former Raider p.r. man Lee Grosscup once said, seriously, that Davis had every other AFL team's office bugged. "I want to be candid," Davis said in 1984. "We do have contacts at every level, on every team." The NFL handled Davis with caution, if not outright fear. In 1983, in the middle of his ugly litigation with the NFL, Davis acquired cornerback Mike Haynes from the Patriots for a first-round draft choice. Haynes's agent, Howard Slusher, recalls: "One of the league lawyers said, 'What if Al refuses to give the pick?' But that wasn't the height of the paranoia. That came when my 15-year-old son, John, went downstairs to Xerox the new contract. Two NFL guys went with him. They didn't want to let the contract out of their sight."

Once, when Harland Svare was coaching San Diego and the Chargers came to Oakland for a game, the rumor was that Davis had bugged the visitors' locker room. Svare looked up at a light fixture and said, "Damn you, Al Davis, damn you. I know you're up there."

"Ah, hell," said Davis, hearing that one. "It wasn't in the light fixture."

Architects

SID GILLMAN

Odd choice. He was a successful but not boffo head coach for San Diego and Houston of the AFL and NFL. Indeed, he was more famous as a college college than as a pro coach. But wait. Listen to three stories.

A young coach from St. Cecilia's High School in Englewood, N.J., Vince Lombardi, visited the line coach at Army, Sid Gillman, several times in the late '40s. Lombardi took Gillman's job in 1949 when Gillman moved to the University of Cincinnati as head coach. Gillman taught Lombardi to study film. He taught him technical line blocking—to take the defender in the direction he's already going and let the back run to the biggest hole he sees. In *Instant Replay*, his book about life with the Packers, Jerry Kramer wrote, "The West Point players had credited [Gillman] with introducing practice films and game grades at the military academy, and Vince brought those ideas to the Green Bay Packers." The league got to know Lombardi's rushing style as "run to daylight."

When Bill Walsh was an assistant with the Raiders in 1966, he checked into a hotel and flipped on the TV. There was San Diego Charger head coach Sid Gillman at a film projector, lecturing on the technical aspects of coaching the slant pattern. "That day," Walsh recalled, "I realized how technically perfect you could be as a coach. I watched the TV that day, Sid telling the audience just what he'd tell the players or the coaches, and I thought I was watching the master." Walsh turned to Gillman for advice throughout his career, and it was Gillman who persuaded Walsh to deal for Steve Young in 1987.

"When I signed with the USFL in 1984," Young recalls, "I went to Los Angeles and there was this old man helping [head coach] John Hadl coach the offense. It's Sid Gillman. He was a tremendous influence on my career. He would coach all day and then watch film with us late in the afternoon. Finally, early in the evening, I would notice him nodding off, which is pretty normal for a 70-something-year-old guy. So I'd drive him home, and he would be back at it the next day, teaching me everything I need to know to be a pro quarterback."

"If I could remember one-tenth of what he taught me, I'd be a genuis myself," said Ron Jaworski, the former Philadelphia quarterback after spending three hours one afternoon watching films with Gillman.

"Every major-college pass offense, and a lot of those in the NFL, stem from the Gillman system," Al Davis says.

The principles of the system: Have your offensive linemen block the defensive linemen in whatever direction the defenders are rushing. Have your backs break off the block in whatever direction is most open. If your quarterback has a quick release, throw a lot. Train your quarterback to see all his receivers and to bounce on his feet so he's able to throw in any direction in a split-second. Take chances. Throw deep. Spread the field for the defense. Force defenders to cover more ground. Attack. Attack.

And learn. Learn. In the early '90s, coaches were still calling, and Gillman wanted to be on top of everything, even when he was only watching film and critiquing an occasional quarterback. Gillman's influence permeates modern football history, and he, more than any single man, has shaped the offensive game that we watch in record numbers every autumn Sunday.

"If there's anything new in the game," Gillman said, "I want to know about it."

He said that in 1991. At 79.

Architects

BILL WALSH

It bugged Bill Walsh, being in the broadcast booth for NBC between lives. It bugged him to watch NFL teams doing all the things he had taught so many players and coaches to do.

Walsh yearned for the game back then, in 1991. He longed to teach what he'd learned about offensive football and dealing with players and organizing a team. He felt he'd been plunked down in the wrong life, and if he didn't do something about it fast, if he didn't stop trying to get into *USA Today* with some idiotic one-liner to prove he was making progress as an NFL analyst, well ... well, he would feel pretty small and unimportant.

"Substance is not a major part of broadcasting," he said soon after leaving that business. "I am a man who draws pass patterns on his wife's shoulder. I was missing the aesthetic end of the art form I'd spent 20 years developing. My offensive system was the essence of my recognition and feeling of accomplishment, and to step away from that and have it become someone else's ... I watched with envy. I watched with a sense of this being plagiarism."

Life for Walsh was coaching and organizing and building a team. So in 1992 he went back to running a program, at Stanford, where he'd coached in the '70s. But if anything, the move only served to strengthen Walsh's ties to the pro game, because now he was teaching his offense to more people. And he was advising more people in the NFL than when he'd transformed the 49ers into the best team in recent NFL history. Look at the Walsh family tree and its branches spreading all around the league. Look at how many people are running their offense the Bill Walsh way.

In Denver former Stanford assistant Jim Fassel is the first-year offensive coordinator, and he is moving the Broncos toward a controlled passing game. In Washington, Rod Dowhower, out from under the shadow of Joe Gibbs, now controls the offense and has moved the Redskins toward the short-passing system Walsh developed; Dowhower coached under Walsh at Stanford from 1977 to '79. And in Tampa, Sam Wyche, who played for Walsh in Cincinnati and cut his pro coaching teeth under him in San Francisco, runs the offense the Walsh way, as does Bruce Coslet—a former 49er coach under Walsh—with the Jets.

Then there's San Francisco. When Mike Shanahan took the offensive coordinator's job with the 49ers, he watched Walsh's old instructional films on coaching an offense; under Shanahan the 49er offense is a mirror of what it was under Walsh. The same is true in Green Bay, where head coach Mike Holmgren was Walsh's pet pupil with the 49ers in the '80s. And in Minnesota, where head coach Dennis Green, who coached under Walsh for two different stints, with the 49ers and at Stanford in 1977 and '78, is doing many of the things Walsh preaches. One more: Staid Marty Schottenheimer has handed complete control of the Chiefs' offense to Walsh disciple Paul Hackett, with former Walsh quarterback Joe Montana running the system on the field.

And on it goes. The Cleveland draft room is run these days by Mike Lombardi, a scout who watched Walsh weave his magic in the 1986 draft, when he traded down six times to get core players for his third Super Bowl team and also positioned himself to trade for Steve Young in 1987. The 49ers have a vault of Walsh teaching tapes, which they lend to college coaches who want to learn the Walsh, and 49er, way. Even if he is spending his weekends in Corvallis or Palo Alto or Pullman, Walsh is still very much a part of pro football. And he will be for years to come.

CURLY LAMBEAU

There is only room for eight architects of professional football in this book, the editor says. The final spot comes down to, among others, Tex Schramm, the kingmaker of perhaps the most popular franchise in all of sports; Lamar Hunt, who founded the American Football League and pushed it toward merger with the NFL; and Don Shula, who will become the winningest coach of all time some day soon.

I picked Curly Lambeau.

The editor says: "You've got some explaining to do."

Here goes.

Lambeau made football exciting. He was the first pro coach to put on a wide-open aerial show, and a winning aerial show at that. He thought fans deserved to see a wide-open game, not a conservative one. At the age of 23 Lambeau saw the league revoke the Packers' franchise because they had illegally used college players under assumed names; he spearheaded the drive to raise money to get the team back. He made small-town America a fixture in the corporate, big-city NFL. Pro football's development as an egalitarian organization is due largely to Lambeau's efforts: The Packers have twice won three NFL titles in a row (from 1929 to '31 and again from 1965 to '67), something no other team has ever done. Lambeau laid the groundwork for the smallest franchise in the league to win more titles than any other team.

In 1919 Lambeau was a 21-year-old blue-collar guy at the Indian Packing Company in Green Bay. He asked the owner of the company, Frank Peck, for $500 to sponsor the team, offering to call it the Packers so Peck could get some free advertising out of the deal. Fine, Peck said. With Lambeau at quarterback, the Packers went 10–1 that season, winning by an average score—and this is

not a misprint—of 51–1. That season the Packers took a road trip to the Wisconsin hamlet of Ishpeming to play the local team. On each of the game's first three running plays, a Packer went down with a broken bone. So Green Bay went to the air the rest of the day and won 33–0. "That's when I learned the value of the forward pass," Lambeau told Arthur Daley of *The New York Times* years later.

Lambeau went 212-106-21 in his 29 seasons as the Packers' coach. He implemented and polished the Packer offense that featured Don Hutson putting up such ridiculously gaudy numbers; Hutson caught 74 balls for 1,211 yards ... in 1942! In one off-season Lambeau dealt for three players—Cal Hubbard, Johnny Blood and Mike Michalske—who became the backbone of Green Bay's first threepeat team. And Lambeau was tough. Lombardi-tough. One day four of his players reported to practice late. There was an automatic fine of $500 for missing practice, and Lambeau decided to assess the weighty fine on all four guys. He ordered all four to write checks for $500 to the Packers on the spot.

"I'm cashing them, too," he said, "before you can stop payment."

"If you do, I'll kill you," one of the offenders snarled.

"Wouldn't do any good," Lambeau said. "I'll just hit you with another $500 fine."

In 1962, three years before he died, Lambeau watched his old team play the New York Giants at Yankee Stadium for the NFL championship. The Packers dominated the Giants for the second straight season, winning 16–7 before a crowd of 64,892. Not that many people lived in Green Bay. The small-town boy had done pretty darn well for himself, hadn't he?

THE FUTURE

THIS IS WHAT WE KNOW ABOUT
THE FUTURE OF PRO FOOTBALL:
DALLAS COACH JIMMY JOHNSON
HAS SHOWN US THE FUTURE,
and it is rooted not in brawn but in brains. There
are no more secrets. Coaches will have to trust
their judgment, their knowledge of the game and
their ability to motivate people. You have to look
at the game and decide how to win that season
and not be married to some out-of-fashion trend
or quarterback. Johnson and Cowboy owner Jerry
Jones eschewed the conventional NFL wisdom
that stresses the importance of continuity, making
47 trades in their first 38 months on the job. They
signed rookies early. They played more players in
quality time than anyone before them. They scru-
tinized the pro football landscape, developed a
plan and acquired players to make it work, all the
while keeping one eye trained on the future. It's
corny but true: If the guy in the next franchise is
matching you by working 16 hours a day, you'd
better be smarter than he is. The best coaches in
football today are some of the most intelligent:
Johnson, Mike Holmgren, Dennis Green, Bobby
Ross, George Seifert. Isn't it amazing to think
that 18 years ago the Rams didn't hire Bill Walsh
because they thought him too cerebral? Now
seven of Walsh's protégés are NFL head coaches,
and he has gone back to academia.

The game will be ruled by television, pretty
much as it is now. But cable will be a stronger
force than ever before. Pay-per-view will be
introduced by the year 2000, making it possible
for the fan to pay $15 any week and watch any
game currently playing on one of the cable-TV
stations. So don't be surprised if future rule
changes favor the offense. TV loves points.

Of course, there will be teams in Europe—perhaps even in Asia. International expansion is a
given. London, Berlin, Frankfurt—all of them
could sell out NFL games every week. When the
World League was dying a couple of years ago,
Frankfurt general manager Oliver Luck was
painfully chagrined. His team, a loser, was draw-
ing more than 45,000 fans a game to behold this

strange American mixture of sport, sex and rock music. Incredibly, Luck's losing football team was outdrawing one of the best soccer teams in Germany—whose stadium they borrowed—and rocking it with a much younger crowd. "God, don't the owners see what's happening over here?" said a disbelieving Luck. "This thing is hot. It's working. These people are dying for American football." Early next century they ought to get the real stuff.

Make no mistake. The game will be huge. The new free-agency system still has some kinks, but football is the only one of the major sports that appears to have guaranteed itself peaceful labor relations for the rest of the century. That means no work stoppages and no major changes, just the profitable status quo: attendance at NFL games hovering at 90% of capacity and 120 million people watching the Super Bowl on TV.

The sport that paid Pudge Heffelfinger $500 a game a century ago is bigger than ever, and we love it. We must. Look at all the families in their living rooms every fall Sunday, glued to the electronic hearth. Football is our game.

THE SUPER BOWL

RESULTS

	Date	Winner (Share)	Loser (Share)	Score	Site (Attendance)
I	1-15-67	Green Bay ($15,000)	Kansas City ($7,500)	35-10	Los Angeles (61,946)
II	1-14-68	Green Bay ($15,000)	Oakland ($7,500)	33-14	Miami (75,546)
III	1-12-69	NY Jets ($15,000)	Baltimore ($7,500)	16-7	Miami (75,389)
IV	1-11-70	Kansas City ($15,000)	Minnesota ($7,500)	23-7	New Orleans (80,562)
V	1-17-71	Baltimore ($15,000)	Dallas ($7,500)	16-13	Miami (79,204)
VI	1-16-72	Dallas ($15,000)	Miami ($7,500)	24-3	New Orleans (81,023)
VII	1-14-73	Miami ($15,000)	Washington ($7,500)	14-7	Los Angeles (90,182)
VIII	1-13-74	Miami ($15,000)	Minnesota ($7,500)	24-7	Houston (71,882)
IX	1-12-75	Pittsburgh ($15,000)	Minnesota ($7,500)	16-6	New Orleans (80,997)
X	1-18-76	Pittsburgh ($15,000)	Dallas ($7,500)	21-17	Miami (80,187)
XI	1-9-77	Oakland ($15,000)	Minnesota ($7,500)	32-14	Pasadena (103,438)
XII	1-15-78	Dallas ($18,000)	Denver ($9,000)	27-10	New Orleans (75,583)
XIII	1-21-79	Pittsburgh ($18,000)	Dallas ($9,000)	35-31	Miami (79,484)
XIV	1-20-80	Pittsburgh ($18,000)	Los Angeles ($9,000)	31-19	Pasadena (103,985)
XV	1-25-81	Oakland ($18,000)	Philadelphia ($9,000)	27-10	New Orleans (76,135)
XVI	1-24-82	San Francisco ($18,000)	Cincinnati ($9,000)	26-21	Pontiac (81,270)
XVII	1-30-83	Washington ($36,000)	Miami ($18,000)	27-17	Pasadena (103,667)
XVIII	1-22-84	LA Raiders ($36,000)	Washington ($18,000)	38-9	Tampa (72,920)
XIX	1-20-85	San Francisco ($36,000)	Miami ($18,000)	38-16	Stanford (84,059)
XX	1-26-86	Chicago ($36,000)	New England ($18,000)	46-10	New Orleans (73,818)
XXI	1-25-87	NY Giants ($36,000)	Denver ($18,000)	39-20	Pasadena (101,063)
XXII	1-31-88	Washington ($36,000)	Denver ($18,000)	42-10	San Diego (73,302)
XXIII	1-22-89	San Francisco ($36,000)	Cincinnati ($18,000)	20-16	Miami (75,129)
XXIV	1-28-90	San Francisco ($36,000)	Denver ($18,000)	55-10	New Orleans (72,919)
XXV	1-27-91	NY Giants ($36,000)	Buffalo ($18,000)	20-19	Tampa (73,813)
XXVI	1-26-92	Washington ($36,000)	Buffalo ($18,000)	37-24	Minneapolis (63,130)
XXVII	1-31-93	Dallas ($36,000)	Buffalo ($18,000)	52-17	Pasadena (98,374)

MOST VALUABLE PLAYERS

		Position			Position
I	Bart Starr, Green Bay	Quarterback	XIV	Terry Bradshaw, Pittsburgh	Quarterback
II	Bart Starr, Green Bay	Quarterback	XV	Jim Plunkett, Oakland	Quarterback
III	Joe Namath, New York Jets	Quarterback	XVI	Joe Montana, San Francisco	Quarterback
IV	Len Dawson, Kansas City	Quarterback	XVII	John Riggins, Washington	Running Back
V	Chuck Howley, Dallas	Linebacker	XVIII	Marcus Allen, Los Angeles Raiders	Running Back
VI	Roger Staubach, Dallas	Quarterback	XIX	Joe Montana, San Francisco	Quarterback
VII	Jake Scott, Miami	Safety	XX	Richard Dent, Chicago	Defensive End
VIII	Larry Csonka, Miami	Running Back	XXI	Phil Simms, New York Giants	Quarterback
IX	Franco Harris, Pittsburgh	Running Back	XXII	Doug Williams, Washington	Quarterback
X	Lynn Swann, Pittsburgh	Wide Receiver	XXIII	Jerry Rice, San Francisco	Wide Receiver
XI	Fred Biletnikoff, Oakland	Wide Receiver	XXIV	Joe Montana, San Francisco	Quarterback
XII	Randy White, Dallas	Defensive Tackle	XXV	Ottis Anderson, New York Giants	Running Back
	Harvey Martin, Dallas	Defensive End	XXVI	Mark Rypien, Washington	Quarterback
XIII	Terry Bradshaw, Pittsburgh	Quarterback	XXVII	Troy Aikman, Dallas	Quarterback

	W	L	Pct	Pts	Opp Pts
Pittsburgh Steelers	4	0	1.000	103	73
San Francisco 49ers	4	0	1.000	139	63
Green Bay Packers	2	0	1.000	68	24
New York Giants	2	0	1.000	59	39
Chicago Bears	1	0	1.000	46	10
New York Jets	1	0	1.000	16	7
Oakland/Los Angeles Raiders	3	1	.750	111	66
Washington Redskins	3	2	.600	122	103
Baltimore Colts	1	1	.500	23	29
Dallas Cowboys	3	3	.500	164	102
Kansas City Chiefs	1	1	.500	33	42
Miami Dolphins	2	3	.400	74	103
Los Angeles Rams	0	1	.000	19	31
New England Patriots	0	1	.000	10	46
Philadelphia Eagles	0	1	.000	10	27
Cincinnati Bengals	0	2	.000	37	46
Buffalo Bills	0	3	.000	60	109
Denver Broncos	0	4	.000	50	163
Minnesota Vikings	0	4	.000	34	95

CAREER LEADERS

Passing

	GP	Att	Comp	Pct Comp	Yds	Avg Gain	TD	Pct TD	Int	Pct Int	Lg	Rating Pts
Joe Montana, San Francisco	4	122	83	68.0	1142	9.36	11	9.0	0	0.0	44	127.8
Jim Plunkett, Los Angeles Raiders	2	46	29	63.0	433	9.41	4	8.7	0	0.0	t80	122.8
Terry Bradshaw, Pittsburgh	4	84	49	58.3	932	11.10	9	10.7	4	4.8	t75	112.8
Bart Starr, Green Bay	2	47	29	61.7	452	9.62	3	6.4	1	2.1	t62	106.0
Roger Staubach, Dallas	4	98	61	62.2	734	7.49	8	8.2	4	4.1	t45	95.4
Len Dawson, Kansas City	2	44	28	63.6	353	8.02	2	4.5	2	4.5	t46	84.8
Bob Griese, Miami	3	41	26	63.4	295	7.20	1	2.4	2	4.9	t28	72.7
Dan Marino, Miami	1	50	29	58.0	318	6.36	1	2.0	2	4.0	30	66.9
Joe Theismann, Washington	2	58	31	53.4	386	6.66	2	3.4	4	6.9	60	57.1
Jim Kelly, Buffalo	3	95	50	52.6	569	5.99	2	2.1	6	6.3	61	51.6
John Elway, Denver	3	101	46	45.5	669	6.62	2	1.9	6	5.9	t56	49.5

Note: Minimum 40 attempts.

Rushing

	GP	Yds	Att	Avg	Lg	TD
Franco Harris, Pittsburgh	4	354	101	3.5	25	4
Larry Csonka, Miami	3	297	57	5.2	9	2
John Riggins, Washington	2	230	64	3.6	43	2
Timmy Smith, Washington	1	204	22	9.3	58	2
Roger Craig, San Francisco	3	198	52	3.8	18	2
Marcus Allen, Los Angeles Raiders	1	191	20	9.6	t74	2
Thurman Thomas, Buffalo	3	167	36	4.6	31	3
Tony Dorsett, Dallas	2	162	31	5.2	29	1
Mark van Eeghen, Oakland	2	148	36	4.1	11	0
Rocky Bleier, Pittsburgh	4	144	44	3.3	18	0

Receiving

	GP	No.	Yds	Avg	Lg	TD
Andre Reed, Buffalo	3	21	248	11.8	40	0
Roger Craig, San Francisco	3	20	212	10.6	40	2
Jerry Rice, San Francisco	2	18	363	20.2	44	4
Lynn Swann, Pittsburgh	4	16	364	22.8	t64	3
Chuck Foreman, Minnesota	3	15	139	9.3	26	0
Cliff Branch, Los Angeles Raiders	3	14	181	12.9	50	3
Preston Pearson, Balt-Pitt-Dall	5	12	105	8.8	14	0
John Stallworth, Pittsburgh	4	11	268	24.4	t75	3
Dan Ross, Cincinnati	1	11	104	9.5	16	2
Gary Clark, Washington	2	10	169	16.9	34	2

Scoring

	Pts
Roger Craig: XIX, San Francisco vs Miami (1 Run, 2 Pass)	18
Jerry Rice: XXIV, San Francisco vs Denver (3 Pass)	18
Don Chandler: II, Green Bay vs Oakland (3 PAT, 4 FG)	15

Rushing Yards

	Yds
Timmy Smith: XXII, Washington vs Denver	204
Marcus Allen: XVIII, LA Raiders vs Washington	191
John Riggins: XVII, Washington vs Miami	166
Franco Harris: IX, Pittsburgh vs Minnesota	158
Larry Csonka: VIII, Miami vs Minnesota	145
Clarence Davis: XI, Oakland vs Minnesota	137
Thurman Thomas: XXV, Buffalo vs NY Giants	135
Matt Snell: III, NY Jets vs Baltimore	121

Receptions

	No.
Dan Ross: XVI, Cincinnati vs San Francisco	11
Jerry Rice: XXIII, San Francisco vs Cincinnati	11
Tony Nathan: XIX, Miami vs San Francisco	10
Ricky Sanders: XXII, Washington vs Denver	9
George Sauer: III, NY Jets vs Baltimore	8
Roger Craig: XXIII, San Francisco vs Cincinnati	8
Andre Reed: XXV, Buffalo vs NY Giants	8
Andre Reed: XXVII, Buffalo vs Dallas	8

Touchdown Passes

	No.
Joe Montana: XXIV, San Francisco vs Denver	5
Terry Bradshaw: XIII, Pittsburgh vs Dallas	4
Doug Williams: XXII, Washington vs Denver	4
Troy Aikman: XXVII, Dallas vs Buffalo	4
Roger Staubach: XIII, Dallas vs Pittsburgh	3
Jim Plunkett: XV, Oakland vs Philadelphia	3
Joe Montana: XIX, San Francisco vs Miami	3
Phil Simms: XXI, NY Giants vs Denver	3

Receiving Yards

	Yds
Jerry Rice: XXIII, San Francisco vs Cincinnati	215
Ricky Sanders: XXII, Washington vs Denver	193
Lynn Swann: X, Pittsburgh vs Dallas	161
Andre Reed: XXVII, Buffalo vs Dallas	152
Jerry Rice: XXIV, San Francisco vs Denver	148
Max McGee: I, Green Bay vs Kansas City	138
George Sauer: III, NY Jets vs Baltimore	133

Passing Yards

	Yds
Joe Montana: XXIII, San Francisco vs Cincinnati	357
Doug Williams: XXII, Washington vs Denver	340
Joe Montana: XIX, San Francisco vs Miami	331
Terry Bradshaw: XIII, Pittsburgh vs Dallas	318
Dan Marino: XIX, Miami vs San Francisco	318
Terry Bradshaw: XIV, Pittsburgh vs LA Rams	309
John Elway: XXI, Denver vs NY Giants	304
Ken Anderson: XVI, Cincinnati vs San Francisco	300

ALL-TIME NFL LEADERS

Scoring

	Yrs	TD	FG	PAT	Pts
George Blanda	26	9	335	943	2002
Jan Stenerud	19	0	373	580	1699
Pat Leahy	18	0	304	558	1470
Jim Turner	16	1	304	521	1439
Mark Moseley	16	0	300	482	1382
Jim Bakken	17	0	282	534	1380
Nick Lowery	14	0	306	449	1367
Fred Cox	15	0	282	519	1365
Lou Groza	17	1	234	641	1349
Jim Breech	14	0	243	517	1246
Chris Bahr	14	0	241	490	1213
Matt Bahr	14	0	237	431	1142
Gino Cappelletti	11	42	176	350	1130
Gary Anderson	11	0	258	356	1130
Ray Wersching	15	0	222	456	1122
Eddie Murray	12	0	244	381	1113
Morten Andersen	11	0	246	347	1085
Don Cockroft	13	0	216	432	1080
Garo Yepremian	14	0	210	444	1074
Bruce Gossett	11	0	219	374	1031

Cappelletti's total includes four two-point conversions.

Rushing

	GP	ATT	YDS	AVG	LG	TD
Walter Payton	13	3,838	16,726	4.4	76	110
Eric Dickerson	10	2,970	13,168	4.4	85	90
Tony Dorsett	12	2,936	12,739	4.3	99	77
Jim Brown	9	2,359	12,312	5.2	80	106
Franco Harris	13	2,949	12,120	4.1	75	91
John Riggins	14	2,916	11,352	3.9	66	104
O. J. Simpson	11	2,404	11,236	4.7	94	61
Ottis Anderson	14	2,562	10,273	4.0	76	81
Earl Campbell	8	2,187	9,407	4.3	81	74
Jim Taylor	10	1,941	8,597	4.4	84	83
Marcus Allen	11	2,090	8,545	4.1	61	79
Joe Perry	14	1,737	8,378	4.8	78	53
Gerald Riggs	10	1,989	8,188	4.2	58	69
Larry Csonka	11	1,891	8,081	4.3	54	64
Freeman McNeil	12	1,798	8,074	4.5	69	38
Roger Craig	10	1,953	8,070	4.1	71	55
James Brooks	12	1,685	7,962	4.7	65	49
Mike Pruitt	11	1,844	7,378	4.0	77	51
Leroy Kelly	10	1,727	7,274	4.2	70	74
George Rogers	7	1,692	7,176	4.2	79	54

Touchdowns

	YRS	RUSH	PASS REC	RET	TOTAL TD
Jim Brown	9	106	20	0	126
Walter Payton	13	110	15	0	125
John Riggins	14	104	12	0	116
Lenny Moore	12	63	48	2	113
Jerry Rice	8	5	103	0	108
Don Hutson	11	3	99	3	105
Steve Largent	14	1	100	0	101
Franco Harris	13	91	9	0	100
Marcus Allen	10	79	18	1	98
Eric Dickerson	10	90	6	0	96
Jim Taylor	10	83	10	0	93
Tony Dorsett	12	77	13	1	91
Bobby Mitchell	11	18	65	8	91
Leroy Kelly	10	74	13	3	90
Charley Taylor	13	11	79	0	90
Don Maynard	15	0	88	0	88
Lance Alworth	11	2	85	0	87
Paul Warfield	13	1	85	0	86
Ottis Anderson	13	81	5	0	86
Tommy McDonald	12	0	84	1	85

Combined Yards Gained

	YRS	TOTAL	RUSH	REC	INT RET	PUNT RET	KICKOFF RET	FUM RET
Walter Payton	13	21,803	16,726	4,538	0	0	539	0
Tony Dorsett	12	16,326	12,739	3,554	0	0	0	33
Jim Brown	9	15,459	12,312	2,499	0	0	648	0
Eric Dickerson	10	15,262	13,168	2,079	0	0	0	15
James Brooks	12	14,644	7,962	3,621	0	565	2,762	0
Franco Harris	13	14,622	12,120	2,287	0	0	233	−18
O.J. Simpson	11	14,368	11,236	2,142	0	0	990	0
James Lofton	15	14,094	246	13,821	0	0	0	27
Bobby Mitchell	11	14,078	2,735	7,954	0	699	2,690	0
John Riggins	14	13,435	11,352	2,090	0	0	0	−7
Steve Largent	14	13,396	83	13,089	0	68	156	0
Ottis Anderson	14	13,364	10,273	3,062	0	0	0	29
Greg Pruitt	12	13,262	5,672	3,069	0	2,007	2,514	0
Ollie Matson	14	12,884	5,173	3,285	51	595	3,746	34
Roger Craig	10	12,812	8,070	4,742	0	0	0	0
Marcus Allen	11	12,803	8,545	4,258	0	0	0	0

Combined Yards Gained – (Continued)

	Yrs	Total	Rush	Rec	Int Ret	Punt Ret	Kickoff Ret	Fum Ret
Tim Brown	10	12,684	3,862	3,399	0	639	4,781	3
Lenny Moore	12	12,451	5,174	6,039	0	56	1,180	2
Don Maynard	15	12,379	70	11,834	0	132	343	0
Charlie Joiner	18	12,367	22	12,146	0	0	194	5

Passing

	Yrs	Att	Comp	Pct Comp	Yds	Avg Gain	TD	Pct TD	Int	Pct Int	Rating Pts
Joe Montana	13	4,600	2,929	63.7	35,124	7.64	244	5.3	123	2.7	93.5
Steve Young	8	1,506	908	60.3	11,877	7.89	76	5.0	42	2.8	90.4
Dan Marino	10	5,284	3,128	59.2	39,502	7.48	290	5.5	165	3.1	87.8
Jim Kelly	7	3,024	1,824	60.3	23,031	7.62	161	5.3	108	3.6	86.9
Mark Rypien	5	1,888	1,078	57.1	14,414	7.63	97	5.1	65	3.4	84.3
Roger Staubach	11	2,958	1,685	57.0	22,700	7.67	153	5.2	109	3.7	83.4
Neil Lomax	8	3,153	1,817	57.6	22,771	7.22	136	4.3	90	2.9	82.7
Sonny Jurgensen	18	4,262	2,433	57.1	32,224	7.56	255	6.0	189	4.4	82.6
Len Dawson	19	3,741	2,136	57.1	28,711	7.67	239	6.4	183	4.9	82.6
Dave Krieg	13	3,989	2,326	58.3	29,247	7.33	210	5.3	160	4.0	82.1
Ken Anderson	16	4,475	2,654	59.3	32,838	7.34	197	4.4	160	3.6	81.9
Boomer Esiason	9	3,378	1,897	56.2	25,671	7.60	174	5.2	129	3.8	81.8
Bernie Kosar	8	3,012	1,174	58.9	21,097	7.00	111	3.7	78	2.6	81.8
Danny White	13	2,950	1,761	59.7	21,959	7.44	155	5.3	132	4.5	81.7
Ken O'Brien	9	3,465	2,039	58.8	24,386	7.04	124	3.6	95	2.7	81.0
Warren Moon	9	4,026	2,329	57.8	30,200	7.50	175	4.3	145	3.6	81.0
Bart Starr	16	3,149	1,808	57.4	24,718	7.85	152	4.8	138	4.4	80.5
Fran Tarkenton	18	6,467	3,686	57.0	47,003	7.27	342	5.3	266	4.1	80.4
Dan Fouts	15	5,604	3,297	58.8	43,040	7.68	254	4.5	242	4.3	80.2
Randall Cunningham	8	2,641	1,464	55.4	18,193	6.89	126	4.8	82	3.1	79.9

1,500 or more attempts. The passing ratings are based on performance standards established for completion percentage, interception percentage, touchdown percentage, and average gain. Passers are allocated points according to how their marks compare with those standards.

Receiving

	GP	No.	Yds	Avg	Lg	TD
Art Monk	13	847	11,628	13.7	79	63
Steve Largent	14	819	13,089	16.0	74	100
Charlie Joiner	18	750	12,146	16.2	87	65
James Lofton	15	750	13,821	18.4	80	75
Ozzie Newsome	13	662	7,980	12.1	74	47
Charley Taylor	13	649	9,110	14.0	88	79
Don Maynard	15	633	11,834	18.7	87	88
Raymond Berry	13	631	9,275	14.7	70	68
Jerry Rice	8	610	10,273	16.8	96	103
Drew Hill	13	600	9,447	15.7	81	60
Harold Carmichael	14	590	8,985	15.2	85	79
Fred Biletnikoff	14	589	8,974	15.2	82	76
Harold Jackson	16	579	10,372	17.9	79	76
Lionel Taylor	10	567	7,195	12.7	80	45
Wes Chandler	11	559	8,966	16.0	85	56
Stanley Morgan	14	557	10,716	19.2	76	72
Roy Green	14	559	8,965	16.0	83	66
Mark Clayton	10	550	8,643	15.7	78	81
Roger Craig	10	547	4,742	8.7	73	16
J.T. Smith	13	544	6,974	12.8	77	35

SINGLE-SEASON LEADERS

Scoring

	Year	TD	PAT	FG	Pts
Paul Hornung, Green Bay	1960	15	41	15	176
Mark Moseley, Washington	1983	0	62	33	161
Gino Cappelletti, Boston	1964	7	38	25	155

Scoring (Continued)

	YEAR	TD	PAT	FG	PTS
Chip Lohmiller, Washington	1991	0	56	31	149
Gino Cappelletti, Boston	1961	8	48	17	147
Paul Hornung, Green Bay	1961	10	41	15	146
Jim Turner, New York Jets	1968	0	43	34	145
John Riggins, Washington	1983	24	0	0	144
Kevin Butler, Chicago	1985	0	51	31	144
Tony Franklin, New England	1986	0	44	32	140

Note: Cappelletti's 1964 total includes a two-point conversion.

Rushing

	YEAR	ATT	YDS	AVG
Eric Dickerson, Los Angeles Rams	1984	379	2105	5.6
O. J. Simpson, Buffalo	1973	332	2003	6.0
Earl Campbell, Houston	1980	373	1934	5.2
Jim Brown, Cleveland	1963	291	1883	6.4
Walter Payton, Chicago	1977	339	1852	5.5
Eric Dickerson, Los Angeles Rams	1986	404	1821	4.5
O. J. Simpson, Buffalo	1975	329	1817	5.5
Eric Dickerson, Los Angeles Rams	1983	390	1808	4.6
Marcus Allen, Los Angeles Raiders	1985	390	1759	4.6
Gerald Riggs, Atlanta	1985	397	1719	4.3
Emmitt Smith, Dallas	1992	373	1713	4.6

PASSING

Yards Gained

	YEAR	ATT	COMP	PCT	YDS
Dan Marino, Miami	1984	564	362	64.2	5084
Dan Fouts, San Diego	1981	609	360	59.1	4802
Dan Marino, Miami	1986	623	378	60.7	4746
Dan Fouts, San Diego	1980	589	348	59.1	4715
Warren Moon, Houston	1991	655	404	61.7	4690
Warren Moon, Houston	1990	584	362	62.0	4689
Neil Lomax, St. Louis	1984	560	345	61.6	4614
Lynn Dickey, Green Bay	1983	484	289	59.7	4458
Dan Marino, Miami	1988	606	354	58.4	4434
Bill Kenney, Kansas City	1983	603	346	57.4	4348

Passer Rating

	Year	Rat.
Joe Montana, San Francisco	1989	112.4
Milt Plum, Cleveland	1960	110.4
Sammy Baugh, Washington	1945	109.9
Dan Marino, Miami	1984	108.9
Steve Young, San Francisco	1992	107.0

Touchdowns

	Year	No.
Dan Marino, Miami	1984	48
Dan Marino, Miami	1986	44
George Blanda, Houston	1961	36
Y. A. Tittle, New York Giants	1963	36

RECEIVING

Receptions

	YEAR	No.	YDS
Sterling Sharpe, Green Bay	1992	108	1461
Art Monk, Washington	1984	106	1372
Charley Hennigan, Houston	1964	101	1546
Lionel Taylor, Denver	1961	100	1176
Jerry Rice, San Francisco	1990	100	1502
Haywood Jeffires, Houston	1991	100	1181
Todd Christensen, LA Raiders	1986	95	1153
Johnny Morris, Chicago	1964	93	1200
Al Toon, New York Jets	1988	93	1067
Michael Irvin, Dallas	1991	93	1523
Andre Rison, Atlanta	1992	93	1121

Yards Gained

	YEAR	YDS
Charley Hennigan, Houston	1961	1746
Lance Alworth, San Diego	1965	1602
Jerry Rice, San Francisco	1986	1570
Roy Green, St. Louis	1984	1555

Touchdowns

	YEAR	No.
Jerry Rice, San Francisco	1987	22
Mark Clayton, Miami	1984	18

four tied with 17

PHOTOGRAPHY CREDITS

FRONT COVER
Neil Leifer

BACK COVER
UPI/BETTMANN

FRONT MATTER
1, Hank Walker/LIFE; 2-3, Walter Iooss Jr.

BEGINNINGS
7, HOF/NFL PHOTOS; 8, HOF/NFL PHOTOS; 9, HOF/NFL PHOTOS;

THE ELEMENTS
10-11, John W. McDonough; 12-13, Michael S. Green; 14-15, Walter Iooss Jr.; 16-17, Tony Tomsic; 18-19, Walter Iooss Jr.; 20-21, Walter Iooss Jr.; 22-23, Neil Leifer; 24-25, Walter Iooss Jr.; 26-27, Walter Iooss Jr.; 28-29, THE BETTMAN ARCHIVE INC.; 30-31, Peter Read Miller; 32-33, UPI/BETTMAN; 34-35, John Biever; 36-37, Heinz Kluetmeier; 38-39, Walter Iooss Jr.; 40-41, John G. Zimmerman; 42-43, John W. McDonough;

GAMES
44-45, Neil Leifer; 46-47, AP/Wide World Photos; 48-49, Walter Iooss Jr.; 50-51, Walter Iooss Jr.; 52-53, HOF/NFL PHOTOS; 54-55, Rick Stewart/ALLSPORT; 56-57, UPI/BETTMANN; 58-59, UPI/BETTMANN; 60-61, Ronald C. Modra; 62-63, Heinz Kluetmeier; 64-65, Malcolm Emmons/NFL PHOTOS; 66-67, UPI/BETTMANN; 68-69, Walter Iooss Jr.; 70-71, UPI/BETTMANN; 72-73, Heinz Kluetmeier; 74-75, Russ Reed/NFL PHOTOS; 76-77, Andy Hayt; 78-79, Peter Read Miller; 80-81, Rich Clarkson; 82-83, HOF/NFL PHOTOS; 84-85, UPI/BETTMANN; 86-87, WIDE WORLD PHOTOS/NFL PHOTOS; 88-89, HOF/NFL PHOTOS; 90-91, UPI/BETTMANN/NFL PHOTOS; 92-93, James Drake; 94-95, Walter Iooss Jr.; 96-97, John D. Hanlon NEWSPHOTOS; 105, Leviton-Atlanta;

PLAYERS
98-99, Neil Leifer; 101, Press Association, Inc.; 103, Neil Leifer; 105, Ray Matjasic; 107, Bill Eppridge; 109, Walter Iooss Jr.; 111, Walter Iooss Jr.; 113, Peter Read Miller; 115, John Iacono; 117, Associated Press; 119, UPI/BETTMANN; 121, John Biever; 123, Neil Leifer; 125, Neil Leifer; 127, UPI/BETTMANN; 129, Walter Iooss Jr.; 131, John Iacono; 135, John W. McDonough; 137, John G. Zimmerman; 139, Walter Iooss Jr.; 141, Art Shay; 143, UPI/BETTMANN; 145, Neil Leifer; 147, Walter Iooss Jr.; 149, John Biever; 151, Heinz Kluetmeier; 153, Associated Press; 155, UPI/BETTMANN; 157, AP/WIDE WORLD PHOTOS; 159, John G. Zimmerman; 161, Peter Read Miller; 163, Heinz Kluetmeier; 165, Neil Leifer; 167, John W. McDonough; 169, Fred Kaplan/B.S.

TEAMS
170-171, Neil Leifer; 172-173, Hy Peskin; 174-175, Walter Iooss Jr.; 177, James Drake; 178-179, John Iacono; 180-181, NFL PHOTOS; 182-183, Walter Iooss Jr.; 184-185, HOF/NFL PHOTOS; 186-187, Russ Reed/NFL PHOTOS; 188-189, UPI/BETT-MANN; 191, George Gellantly/NFL PHOTOS.

ARCHITECTS
192-193, UPI/BETTMANN; 195, NFL PHOTOS; 197, NFL PHOTOS; 199, Richard Meek; 201, Tony Triolo; 203, Richard Mackson; 205, Charles Aqua Viva/NFL PHOTOS; 207, Walter Iooss Jr; 209, HOF/NFL PHOTOS.

THE FUTURE
210-211, Jason Shillingford/ACTION PLUS.

Acme Packing Company 185
Alabama, University of 18, 100
Alexander, Joe 26
Alexander, Kermit 90
All America Football Conference 82, 104, 152, 172, 173, 198
Allegheny Athletic Club 6
Allen, George 39, 122, 132
Ameche, Alan 46, *47*, 48
American Football League 66, 75, 173, 175, 200, 202, 208
American Professional Football Association 6, 8, 154, 196
Anderson, Donnie 58
Anderson, Ottis 152

Bachelors III 6
Bahr, Matt 39
Baltimore Colts 46, 48, 49, 50, 110, 132, 146, 164, 176
Banks, Chip 97
Barber, Red 86
Baugh, Sammy 104, 116, **117**, 181
Bear Behind 8
"Bear Down, Chicago Bears" 181
Bednarik, Chuck 126, **127**
Bell, Bert 82, 83, 173, 200
Benirschke, Rolf 62
Bennett, Cornelius 54
Benton, Jim 100
Berchtold, Scott 54, 106
Berry, Raymond 48, 106, 110, 160, 168
Biletnikoff, Fred 76, 168, 186, **187**
Billups, Lewis 78
Blackwood, Lyle 61
Blanda, George 39, 168, **169**, 186, **187**
Bleier, Rocky 94, **95**, 176
Blood, Johnny 138, 168, 189, 208
Bloomfield Rams 110
Blount, Mel 124
Bond, James 186
Bonds, Barry 102
Boston Braves 154
Braase, Ordell 26, **27**
Bradshaw, Terry 63, 64, **92**, **93**, 94, 144, **145**, 176
Brooklyn Dodgers 116, 198
Brooks, James 62, 134, 198
Brown, Jim 14, **15**, 100, 102, **103**, 106, 108, 114, 122, 126, 128, 130, 136, 152
Brown, Mike 134
Brown, Paul 14, 82, 83, 104, 134, 152, 173, 198, **199**, 200
Brown, Pete 134
Brown, Tom 66
Brumbaugh, Carl 87
Bryan, Billy 97
Bukich, Rudy 90
Buffalo All-Americans **188**
Buffalo Bills 39, 54, 55, 68, 70, 106, 122, 152, 184
Bugel, Joe 120
Buoniconti, Nick 80, 182, **183**
Burnett, Dale 89
Butkus, Dick 106, **107**, 124, 126, 138, 194
Byrd, Dennis 31

Byrd, Gill 160

Caffey, LeRoy 176
Camp, Walter 14, 17, 18, 19, 22, 32
Candlestick Park 68, 178
Candy, John 78
Canton Bulldogs 154, **184**, **185**, 196
Carlisle Indian School 35, 154
Carr, Joe 51, 185, 196, **197**
Catholic Voice, The 168
Cavanaugh, Matt 178
Chamberlain, Guy 185
Chamberlain, Wilt 100
Cherry, Deron 160
Chicago Bears 9, 35, 40, 51, 52, 71, 72, 84, 86, 87, 106, 116, 118, 124, 142, 150, 162, 166, 172, 176, **180**, **181**, 185, 189, 194, 196
Chicago Cardinals 71, 92, 154, 156, 185
Chicago Cubs 89
Chicago Stadium 118, 180
Chicago Staleys 185
Chicago Tribune, 26
Christie, Steve **54**, 55
Cincinnati Bengals 23, 77, 78, 112, 134, 198, 206
Cincinnati Reds 154
Cincinnati, University of 204
Clack, Jim 176
Clark, Dutch 180
Clark, Dwight 112, 178
Cleveland Browns 46, 49, 82, 83, 92, 95, 97, 100, 104, 120, 122, 126, 130, 140, 152, 166, 168, **172**, **173**, 178, 182, 190, 198, 202, 206
Cline, Ollie 190, **191**
Collinsworth, Cris 78
Conn, Tuffy 31
Coolidge, President Calvin 9, 142
Corbett, George 87
Cosell, Howard 164
Coslet, Bruce 206
Costner, Kevin 196
Cotton Bowl 112
Country Joe and the Fish 49
Craig, Roger 14, **78**, 79, 108, 178, 179
Cross, Randy 78, 198
Csonka, Larry 79, 80, **81**, 102, 183
Cubs Park 142
Cunningham, Randall 162, 179

Dale, Carroll 58
Daley, Arthur 208
Dallas Cowboys 35, 41, 56, 58, 73, 74, 93, 122, 130, 144, 166, 175, 178, 179, 182, 186, 210
Davidson, Ben 76
Davis, Al 35, 49, 76, 173, 186, 187, 200, 202, **203**, 204
Davis, Kenneth 55
Davis, Mouse 35
Dawson, Len 66
DeBartolo, Eddie 179
Dempsey, Jack 9, 71, 142
Dent, Richard **34**, 35
Denver Broncos 39, 95, 97, 150, 152, 160, 206

Detroit Lions 35, 104, 106, 118, 156, 173, 190
Dickerson, Eric 114
DiMaggio, Joe 148
Dirty Dozen, The 102
Dishman, Cris 55
Ditka, Mike 94, 108
Donovan, Artie 126
Dorsett, Tony 114
Doubleday, Abner 184
Dowhower, Rod 206
Dowler, Boyd 58, 67
DuPree, Billy Joe 94

Eagle Feather 8
Eller, Carl 150
Ellis, William Webb 13, 14
Elway, John **16**, 17, **96**, 97
Erhardt, Ron 68
Esiason, Boomer 55
Everett, Jim 148
Ewbank, Weeb 46, 110, 146

Fagan, Kevin 178
Fassel, Jim 206
Fears, Tom 156
Fencik, Gary **34**, 35
Fernandez, Manny 182, **183**
Fielder, Cecil 40
Fitzstephen, William 36
Florence Teachers College 194
Flores, Tom 187
Foot Ball: How to Coach a Team 17
Ford, Len 173
Fort Ord 156
Forzano, Rick 130
Fouts, Dan 61, **62**, 63, 148, 162
Frank, John 78
Frankford Yellow Jackets 8, 142, 185, 189
Frankfurt Galaxy (WLAF) 210
Franklin, Andra 62
Fredrickson, Tucker 90
Friesel, Red 86
Fuqua, Frenchy 63, 64
Fulcher, David 78

Galt Ocean Mile Hotel 50
Garrett, Mike 67
Garrison, Walt 73
Gatski, Frank **172**, 173
Gerela, Roy 36, **37**, 63, 138
Giants Stadium 31
Gibbs, Joe 194, 206
Gibron, Abe **172**, 173
Gifford, Frank 46, 126, 132, 175
Gillingham, Gale 58
Gillman, Sid 35, 49, 204, **205**
Givins, Ernest 55
Gogolak, Charlie 39
Gogolak, Pete 39
Golic, Bob 92
Graham, Otto 82, 83, 100, 104, **105**, 106, 112, 130, 152, 160, 173, 190
Grange, Red 6, 8, **9**, 26, **28**, **29**, 51, 52, 70, **71**, 72, 87, 89, 90, 118, 142, **143**, 180, 181, 189, 194, 196
Green Bay Packers 8, 18, 19, 40, 56, 58,